BORN ♥ BLUE

Nicole Ribbens

For my darling Louis,
In pursuit of meaning
For reconciliation
For you
For life.

He who learns must suffer. And even in our sleep pain that cannot forget falls drop by drop upon the heart, and in our own despair, against our will, comes wisdom to us by the awful grace of God.

— Aeschylus

Contents

PART I

Before

Eighteen-year-old me had a plan. Graduate college in four years, get married by twenty-four, have my first baby at twenty-five, and my last baby by twenty-eight. I'd go back to school for a master's degree in art therapy. Certainly, I would work as an art curator while raising my children. I kept planning. My eventual husband would stand tall and strong. Our babies would have blonde curly hair and green eyes and they would sit quietly through church and sleep through the night. Scenes of stability surrounded me. I attended weddings of friends before I could legally toast the happy couple. These accomplishments were tangible. I could reach out and touch them. If I followed their lead, I would find a partner and build a foundation. Nothing about this plan was wildly unreasonable, except me.

College took longer than I expected. Inching toward my first goal with a bachelor's degree in art history, five aimless years passed. Three unpaid internships left me worn down and uninspired. I began cataloging a basement full of maps and photographs, studying images for tiny hints at dates to enter into the Oakland County Pioneer and Historical Society's dinosaur database, researching and rewriting artwork descriptions for the Flint Institute of Arts, peddling memberships, and curating modern art exhibits at the Museum of New Art. I'd start a new role with enthusiasm until it slowly stretched me too thin. Between internships, I worked four part-time jobs. I started shelving books while timing espresso shots at Borders Books. After early mornings at the bookstore, I worked late nights closing the café, wiping counters, and brewing coffee at the Bean & Leaf. When hours thinned out at the coffee shop, I started crafting window displays and taking inventory at Little Monsters Toys. Between classes, I answered front-desk questions at the Oakland University Art Gallery. I kept trail mix and a change of clothes in my car, always driving from one obligation to the next, staying noncommittal to friends.

Every other semester, I dropped my classes to take an extra job to save for the next semester's tuition. Always one step behind, I hoped a break from classes would put me ahead. My friends all went to different schools, so we caught up on weekends. Money stayed tight. I lived paycheck-to-paycheck, hoping friends wouldn't notice me recounting singles from my coffee shop tips to pay for PBR.

Seventy percent of Oakland University's student body commutes from all around metro Detroit. A lonely campus. I wasn't invited to frat parties or study groups. No one stuck around to make friends. I sat in the front row during lectures to keep from being lulled to sleep by the warm hum of the slide projector. Managing night classes and unpaid internships left no time for making new friends.

I put my domestic goals on hold to complete my undergrad, surviving on refried beans and Totino's frozen pizzas. I worked the early shift shelving books in Auburn Hills. That 5 a.m. start meant free coffee before the till hit the cash drawer. That's where I met someone who saw the world differently, someone gentle and reserved. Unassuming, he spoke thoughtfully of his experiences. We got to know each other over Wild Turkey and reruns of The Office with the subtitles on. We read books together, teaching me to slow down and consider each individual word. I became a better reader, more acutely aware of the world around me. We spent most of our time between his parents' house, a home filled with music, and my quiet apartment above the yarn shop, where you could hear the push and pull of the loom on knitting club nights while we ate dinner upstairs.

He held my clammy hand and quelled my self-doubt with reassurance during my capstone lecture on Religious Eschatology and the Nuclear Experience. I wanted to hide in the parking lot until it ended, but he encouraged me to sit and listen to other students, to admire a semester of hard work. Most of all, he shared his adoring family with me, representing a future I could walk toward. Sensitive but not outspoken, he taught me patience. I learned how to speak up, to give volume to my need for emotional support. I thought naming your needs equaled maturity, but that's where our paths diverged.

On a warm day in June, we sat side by side on the hammock I'd tucked between towering pine trees that overlooked the neighboring cemetery. I knew he was searching for something—purpose in his life, meaning in his actions, the words to use so it might hurt less.

"I don't love you the same way you love me," he said. I panicked. Desperate for a resolution that would keep us together, I offered him space.

We sat shoulder to shoulder for what felt like hours. Talking at first, then crying. Eventually, we surrendered to silence as we came to an impasse. I was afraid of what I would feel when I inevitably walked away... I pleaded for compromise, but how could he ignore his insatiable wanderlust? He knew we would never be truly happy if he stayed. I waited in silence for a solution to reveal itself, but it never came. I knew once I left that it would all end. The future I thought I had been walking toward turned into a dead end.

He quit his job and our relationship simultaneously. He kept only what fit in his car: camping equipment, a blue stuffed elephant from his nephew. He left his cat with his parents and sold his bed and dresser. I gave him a book of photos, a final effort to prove my worth. I poured my heart into creating an index of our memories in hopes he might experience a miraculous change of heart. I ignored his barefaced indifference and handed him the book. He flipped through it, thanked me for my thoughtfulness, and handed it back. I refused to give up.

I begged.

He couldn't settle.

I pleaded.

He got in his car.

With no particular purpose in mind, he drove away. I am not sure what hurt more—that he simply didn't love me or that despite not knowing his destination, he knew it wasn't with me.

All the life we lived together. Best friends, soon to be strangers.

Miming the motions of my life, I assured myself he'd return. I stayed upright only long enough to clock in and out of work. At night I'd retreat to my room, praying and pleading and writing down my feelings. I surrounded myself with the people I loved, including his sister and his mother. I held on to a tiny flicker of hope. I wallowed and waited for three months. I cried myself awake for six more. I ate enough to keep my body moving but I never tasted a thing. I learned of his travels from our mutual friends. He was couch-surfing in Memphis, Tennessee, while I prayed for his return. He headed west camping through the Badlands and Yellowstone. It wasn't until he landed in Alaska that I realized he wasn't coming back.

Surrounded by a life we'd built together, swallowed up in the leftovers of our relationship, I decided it was my turn to leave for all the same reasons. Unhappy and stuck, I needed more but I wouldn't go until I had a plan. A destination. I drove across the state to hunt for an apartment and a job. I spent weekdays in metro Detroit and weekends in Grand Rapids, crashing on my cousin Molly's couch. I saved my money. I gave two weeks' notice and left my job. I packed what I needed, sorting my dishes and books into donation piles. I tossed out the remaining photographs of my relationship, evidence of camping trips to the Great Lakes, parties with friends, memories of vacations passed. I finally found a place to live. A second-floor, one-bedroom apartment in an old, drafty house situated two-and-a-half hours west of the heartbreak. It had a closet for a kitchen and a giant porch. The old wood floors, once covered with roofing tar, were stiff and uneven. The landlord could show it to me right away, but I was back home, cleaning out my old apartment, packing up the parts of my life I wanted to keep. I sent Molly to look at it for me. She called right away.

"I am standing on your new balcony. The floors are weird, but you want this apartment. It's a steal."

Her confidence and enthusiasm oozed through the phone.

"I told the landlord you were a librarian and a nanny, and she'd never find a better tenant," Molly continued.

At the high end of what I could afford, especially without a job, I held my breath and signed the twelve-month lease. Tucked into baskets and boxes, haphazard from using my car as a dresser, I unpacked my clothes. The landlord bought a discount rug to cover the worst of the bedroom floor. I brought a hammock for the porch, a box fan for warm summer nights and a full-size bed from my grandmother that landed in the center of the bedroom rug. The only furniture I owned.

It was enough.

A blank slate away from the history of my heartache, the first six months were spent merely climbing out of bed each morning. Making decisions that considered only me, reminding myself that I am resilient and important.

I started exploring the neighborhood one block at a

time, discovering a lunch spot around the corner called Martha's Vineyard. I'd wander the aisles filled with gourmet snacks and still buy the same thing every day: a sundried tomato, basil, and mozzarella sandwich on asiago bread, with spicy pickle chips and a pomegranate San Pellegrino. Then I would drive a mile downtown and sit by the river to eat. The spicy, savory, and sparkling combination tasted of excitement and apprehension.

Free-admission Tuesdays allowed me to take myself on an art museum date to see a familiar photographer's exhibit: Edward Burtynsky: Water. I saw Burtynsky's images once before in an exhibit called Imaging a Shattering Earth at the Oakland University Art Gallery when I worked there in college. It consisted of a collection of photographs representing the environmental impact of the industrial revolution, revealing degradation and irreversible damage. Familiar enough to feel comfortable, but fresh enough to feel like an adventure, this new collection, Water, reflected modern society's relationship with water. I stepped into the first gallery to see the jarring absence of water throughout different parts of the world. Mesmerized by swirling patterns of dried lake beds, both harmful and haunting, I walked into the next gallery to see manufactured waterfront properties, wealth and excess. I turned the corner to be swallowed up by enormous seven-foot aerial landscapes, disorienting and honest, blurring the line where land and sea meet. Assemblage, control, displacement, depletion. I felt it all. I moved between galleries studying every shape and shade until they no longer resembled landscapes. Later, I tucked the exhibit flier on the only shelf in my room.

A souvenir, a physical reminder of my own impact and power.

On a nonexistent budget with no paycheck, I couldn't afford internet in my apartment. I tucked myself into a corner of the library with a wide view of the city to the south, ignoring the other patrons using the same space as their dining and living rooms. I turned a communal table into my personal office, spreading my laptop out next to an open notebook and an eager pen. I spent afternoons scouring the internet for employment. Keyword searches for art, research, writing, museum, curatorial, intern, and library aid returned half a dozen listings. I applied to all of them.

I had an interview at the Children's Museum for something called creative supervisor, a fluffy term for babysitter. I thought the role would allow creative direction with hands-on exhibits and curatorial practice. But during the interview, I learned they would need me to rotate positions throughout my shift—front desk, door greeter, phone reception. Toward the end of my interview, they asked, "Pegasus or unicorn?"

I didn't understand.

"If you could choose one, which would you be?"

I blanked.

He was trying to be playful, but I was serious and needed a job. I could see him eagerly waiting for my reply, so I finally blurted out, "Pegasus! Unicorns can't fly." I left feeling defeated. They never called. I told myself I was overqualified and moved on.

I went back to my comfortable new apartment to take porch naps on my hammock. The trees bent halfway over the balcony creating the perfect pocket of sunlight to sway in and out on warm afternoons. I settled into my new life and all the uncertainty surrounding it.

Just me.

Relief snuck in when I landed a job photographing products for a software company. The job wouldn't start for another six weeks, and I'd be working third shift, but it meant a paycheck and a real job. I wore a dress my first day and immediately regretted it when they handed me a dart gun to start an all-office Nerf war. I felt confident in this creative, albeit silly, environment. I wore jeans every day after that.

Encouraged by my friends back home, I reluctantly downloaded a dating app and swiped left on all the vanity. I managed to drag myself on a few blind dates. I put on a dab of makeup and accepted a dinner invitation. On my first Tinder date, we agreed to meet at Mulligan's, a local bar. I parked my car and walked across the street, stopped by a large group getting on a party bus. The crowd invited me to come with them (absolutely not). One guy stepped off the bus, introduced himself and gave me his number. I crossed the street feeling confident. When I went inside the dimly lit, sticky floored bar, I sat down and scanned the room for my date. The guy next to me bought me a drink while I waited. The first thing my date said was, "You're taller than I expected." We talked about his height insecurity most of the evening while I tried to make myself look smaller. I didn't have the energy to nurture someone else's feelings. I laughed at his stale jokes, inwardly confirming this would be our only date. I blocked his number as soon as I arrived home, alone.

One dating profile, with a short bio that read like a used car ad, caught my attention.

Used 1988 male, comes in all white. Well taken care of with recent body work. Ready for any adventure with a solid navigation system. This model will make you feel comfortable and comes with a good entertainment system. Warning—likes to go fast, be ready to pump the brakes on the downhill. Also, the voice commands don't always work correctly. Clear title!

It made me laugh so I messaged him about his warranty. We exchanged phone numbers and sarcasm for a few days. Smiling at my phone, I agreed to meet for dinner at the end of the week. A few days later, I stopped at the coffee shop where Molly worked. I told her everything I knew about him, his name, phone number, and where we were meeting. I told her if she didn't hear from me by 6:30 p.m., she needed to call the cops. When I showed her his photo, she laughed with relief.

"I know him!"

"He's in here all the time," she said. "He loves the Grateful Dead and always drinks Oolong tea." She peered down the length of the coffee counter to a couple of guys at the opposite end, sipping coffees and pecking away at their laptops.

"Hey guys! My cousin has a Tinder date with Nice Guy Dan. What do you think?"

The two strangers smiled wide and said, "Oh Dan? You'll have a great time!" They introduced themselves and we talked until my coffee ran out. Now I felt more at ease meeting him at a dingy bar in an unfamiliar part of town later that week. And I accidentally made new friends.

On my first date with Nice Guy Dan, I used my phone for directions, landing me in a parking lot twice the size of the bar it advertised—The Rezervoir Lounge. I came in through the back entrance that walked me down a long hallway, opening up into a bar much larger than it appeared from outside. I could feel the smell of stale beer and French fries seeping into my hair. I took a seat at the bar and ordered the only familiar beer on the menu, a Vanilla Java Porter, and waited nervously.

I saw him walk in before he noticed me. He stood taller and thinner than I expected. His dark curly hair sprang up in every direction as he walked assuredly to my side of the bar. He sat down at the stool beside me with a casual hello, as if he were already among friends. No awkward hug or handshake, no silly introduction.

We chatted over the menu. He seemed to know it well. I took his entrée recommendation of a Cajun grilled cheese with fries. I expected generic and clumsy conversation. It wasn't. He was confident, not arrogant, and comfortable in his skin. We talked about our hobbies and details of my new photography job. He told me about his weekly game of badminton at the community gym and the last concert he attended with his brother. Then he hurled a giant, sloppy sneeze into the elbow of his gray dress shirt. He immediately looked down at the bend of his elbow to find bits of sandwich and saliva grinning back at him. It took every ounce of my self-control not to fall out of my stool laughing.

Under his breath, he muttered, "Wow, that was gross." We were elbow-to-elbow and I pretended not to notice his panicked sleeve wiping. I didn't want to further the embarrassment, so I focused on my own plate and stifled my snickers. I changed the subject and we each ordered another beer. He paid our bill and asked if I wanted to go for a walk. It was early in the evening and I liked his company, so I agreed.

We left the dingy bar through the front door and stepped outside, surprised by the glinting evening sun. I took a big, deep breath as I felt the effects of two porters in my belly, then doubled over in laughter, no longer able to ignore the humor of the spit-sneeze. I laughed so hard I couldn't speak. Unbothered by my laughing at him, Dan laughed too.

On our walk, I mentioned how he didn't seem apprehensive and asked how he kept so calm and collected. He told me he always treats first introductions like a reunion with an old friend, that way he avoids nervously saying the wrong thing. We walked around the neighborhood admiring old houses, becoming more comfortable in each other's company. He suggested we catch some live music at a neighboring bar.

After a handful of lousy first dates, I felt surprised at what a nice time the night had turned into. He hopped into my car and gave directions. We listened for a while, but live music doesn't leave room for conversation. When the band took a break, we decided to leave. He asked me If I would drive him home because he had walked from there to the Rez.

When we pulled into the long, narrow driveway

where he lived with a half-dozen roommates, I felt nervous he might invite me in. Instead, he thanked me for a nice evening, hugged me and exited the car. I waited for him to get inside before backing out of his driveway. I made an awkward three-point turn maneuvering my sedan forward and backward between a parked car and a telephone pole—like Austin Powers on a golf cart. I realized he hadn't actually gone inside, but stood at the door watching from the window the entire time.

"He's not calling me after THIS," I muttered as I narrowly missed the telephone pole with my side-view mirror.

Despite my less-than-graceful exit, I left feeling hopeful. Even if the date with Dan didn't turn into another date, I now knew it was possible for me to be vulnerable, to find happiness and forge friendships. Somehow, through heartbreak and the constant emptiness, I started making my own way, putting the pieces of myself back together on my own.

A few days passed and Dan called to say hello. He and his roommates were headed to Vancouver for a trip. He said he'd send photos, and we made plans to meet up once he returned. In the meantime, I deleted my dating apps. Dan and I messaged late into the night during his trip (international rates DO apply between the U.S. and Canada, FYI). When he got back, I came over and joined a euchre game with his friends. They taught me to play, and I assumed I'd be Dan's partner for the tournament. I was surprised to find my partner to be the loudest, most opinionated girl in the room. She introduced herself and said, "You better be good. I came to win!"

At each turn, my palms grew sweatier as I asked clarifying questions before I laid my card, hoping my seasoned teammate approved. Eight hands of euchre later, we came in third place. I survived. And I haven't played euchre since.

Just before the start of my new job, my best friend Lisa came to Grand Rapids to see my new apartment. Armed with family recipes and a carload of groceries, she taught me how to make tortillas, refried beans and rice. My kitchen fit just two people, standing side-by-side. You couldn't open the fridge and stand at the stove at the same time, so we gathered all our ingredients and started to work. She showed me how to mix the dough by hand, with shortening as the secret ingredient. We tore off golf ball-sized rounds of dough and rolled them out with her special rolling pin. She showed me how to perfectly heat the pan to fry the tortilla until it filled with steam, then flip it to brown the other side. I tried my hand at a few before letting her take over. Dan rode his bike over to join us. I had two bar stools at the kitchen counter and no room for a dining table. I bounced between sous chef and hostess while Lisa expertly prepared tortillas and fired questions at Dan: How many siblings did he have? Where did he go to college? Oh, a master's degree? How many roommates did he have? Oh, he owns his house at 26-years-old?

I didn't interrupt the gentle, but pointed, interrogation. I liked watching Lisa look out for me, unearthing details about Dan I didn't know yet while I sat quietly tearing into a warm tortilla. I could barely wait for him to leave before asking for her honest first impression.

With only kind things to say about him, Lisa approved. She liked Dan as much as I did. She tried to act casual when offering her opinion, waiting for the relationship to work itself out, but I could feel her excitement. Dan stayed organized. He had goals and didn't shy away from hard work. He was interesting and funny and easy on the eyes.

I started my job and began working from 8 p.m. to 6 a.m. The schedule made it hard to plan, but Dan and I continued to spend time together. During the week, he would wake up early to make a big breakfast of French toast with his dad's homemade syrup. I would come over at 7 a.m. on my way home from work. We'd eat and then he would go off to work while I went home to sleep.

On weekends, I'd sleep all day Friday to keep normal hours on Saturdays and Sundays. We attended concerts at the Pyramid Scheme and Fred Meijer Gardens. His friends became my friends, inviting me out for happy hour where I started making other friends on my own. His roommates included me in dinner parties and hangouts. I met his sister Rose. She was my age, two years older than Dan, and just as sweet and driven as him.

I introduced Dan to my parents and some extended family during a day trip to my aunt's house on Lake Michigan. We drove the 90 minutes up north to my aunt's property while I warned him about my Uncle Stubby, whose every comment came laced with sarcasm. I felt nervous, but Dan was unrattled by the cuts of crude humor as we sat around the bonfire.

I met his dad and stepmom during dinner at their house. I felt relieved when his sister and her boyfriend, whom I had already met, arrived. Familiar-faced allies. We sat down to dinner and I revealed that I didn't eat meat. Dan's stepmother, Martha, commented on how "Danny always dates girls with specific diets," followed by a trip down memory lane of girlfriends' past. Insecurity crept in. I wondered how many girlfriends there had been before me. I tried not to think about it.

I helped host a Thanksgiving dinner with Dan's siblings and their kids at his house. As the youngest of five, it was a big group. I took the lead on preparing roasted vegetables, carefully washing potatoes and Brussels sprouts while Dan moved pans around to perfect the cooktime for each dish. One of his brothers met me at the kitchen sink. He leaned in and said, "Ya know, I like you. Dan picked a good one." An unexpected and welcome compliment.

On a late fall day, Dan took me for a drive north of town. We parked along a nondescript side street between a few farmhouses and straw fields already harvested for the season. He told me his grandparents used to own this land and it's where his mom grew up. She passed away suddenly when Dan was 22. He and his siblings spread her ashes near the river that ran along the property, a final resting place. I didn't get to meet her, but I felt her there.

A few weeks later, we went to the market to get Dan his first Christmas tree. Six years with his own home and he had never bothered to get a tree! My dad and I built a mantle for my apartment where I could hang Christmas stockings for Dan and me. I couldn't have a Christmas tree in my place, and I refused to spend a winter evening in his living room without the glow of Christmas tree lights. Slowly, Dan's things and my things became our things, events, and friendships, and end tables, too. I took comfort in his bike helmet hanging on my coat rack. With no expectations, we had begun to build a life with one another.

Pregnancy

When the 12-month lease ran out, I moved out of my apartment and into a friend's house. Having roommates meant cheaper rent and lower utilities. Dan helped me move. We loaded our cars and made half a dozen trips across town. I had more furniture this time—a full-size bed and dresser from my grandparents' basement and an Ikea bookshelf I bought with my first paycheck, plus a backseat full of clothes.

I painted my new room a deep gray. I tried to accept that this wasn't a step backward. Cheaper rent was responsible. Maybe I'd get a promotion at work or find a more affordable place in a few months.

My job as a product photographer had me taking pictures of products for retail use, often requiring me to work in-store with products when customers weren't there. My weeks were backward, sl eping when the world worked, working when the world slept. Weekends were sacred. It's the time I used to do all the stuff I couldn't manage during the week. We were nearing a project deadline and needed extra time to complete a shot list. Without anyone else to volunteer, I reluctantly raised my hand. Down the street at our photography studio, I loaded my trunk with the usual photography equipment: studio lights, tripods and backdrops. That's when my supervisor called and asked me to return to the main office. I had wanted to leave early to get a nap in before working all night. Annoyed that I had to make a trip to the office before heading home, I went in expecting to discuss the weekend's task list. He waved me over to the conference room instead. He seemed nervous, putting tension in the air, but I didn't know why. He had me sit down while he paced around the coffee table. And then he said it.

"It just isn't working out."

Confused, I thought he was telling me I was off the hook for working the weekend's overtime.

"It just isn't working out," he repeated.

"Am I... Are you firing me?!" I asked.

He looked me right in the eye and I don't remember what he said next or if he said anything at all. And that was it. I felt the pieces of my life falling away. No job meant no money. I'd have to move out of Grand Rapids and back home to Commerce with my parents. Could I put a hold on my student loans? I'd need to cancel my root canal.

"I can walk you to your car when you're ready," he said. Unsure if he could read how insulting that felt, I gritted my teeth and politely declined. I didn't need to be escorted from the building. I won't make a scene, I thought. I collected my feelings, jamming them into the caverns of my shoes, and took a deep breath. I held my head high and stepped out of the conference room telling myself I only needed to make it to the door, then to the car. I glanced around at my colleagues. Each of them, tucked into their desks, pecking away at their computers like hens, unaware of the seismic earthquake I'd been tossed into.

I slipped out the front door unnoticed and made my way to the parking lot. I still had my keycard. I tried to make a plan. I could return on Saturday to clean out my desk, then I wouldn't have to do it in front of everyone. Safely in my car, I called Dan; my voice barely audible. "I... I just got fired." I started to drive home and remembered my trunk, full of expensive photography equipment, no longer mine. I circled the parking lot and parked again. I closed my eyes and rested my head on the steering wheel. I had to go back to the studio to unload my car before I could climb into bed and cry myself into tomorrow. I walked back into the studio to the surprise of my colleagues: Derek, a fellow photographer; Ian, a project manager; Kara, the creative director; and Lucas, the business manager.

My friends.

My team.

I sat down and cried. They thought I'd been in a car accident. Finally, I found the courage to speak and confirm that there was no accident but I had been fired. I asked Ian to unload my car while I sank deeper into the chair and further into my dread. Kara walked over to me, just as surprised as I was, and hugged me close, my face squeezed against her pregnant belly. We were all stunned. And now they needed to rethink meeting their looming project deadline because I could no longer finish the job. We promised to check in on each other, to stay in touch, before I drove the long two miles home.

Dan rushed over after work where he found me in my room, legs curled into my chest, sniveling into my pillow. He climbed in beside me and stayed quiet until I was ready to talk. He didn't offer any empty advice or look-on-the-bright-side anecdotes. I needed the space to feel sad, and he knew to give me that.

After a week of feeling sorry for myself, I applied for unemployment. I received severance pay from my previous employer, but it barely covered one month's rent after taxes. My savings would have to cover future rents. A little math showed me I could only manage four months of payments with no new income. I applied for ten jobs a week, cataloging each one for the unemployment office. I went to a few interviews. I was either overqualified for an entry-level job or lacked the experience I needed to fit into their niche environments. While I waited for the perfect job to land in my lap, I bled through my savings, facing the serious realization that I may need to move home with my parents.

Some friends suggested I move in with Dan. We'd been together over a year, but I wouldn't consider it. I didn't want the reason we lived together to be out of convenience or necessity, especially because my family wouldn't like the idea without talks of a wedding.

We weren't there yet.

I expected after the holidays I would move back to Commerce, our small hometown about 35 miles outside of Detroit, with my parents. I needed rent-free time to figure out my next steps. Unalarmed by a missed period,

I assumed my body was reacting to stress. I tracked my cycle by the calendar counting back three weeks of cramps and no cycle. I'd never taken a pregnancy test before, but it was worth ruling out. I spent the night at Dan's house to wait out a snowstorm in the middle of a frigid Midwest winter. Two days later, he drove me home on his way to work. Catholics—we don't use birth control or even discuss it in adolescences. As an adult, I never asked. I nervously mentioned my missed period to Dan. A man whose feathers are rarely ruffled, he shrugged with raised eyebrows and offered to take me to the pharmacy. I assured him buying the test was something I could manage on my own. The rest would require a larger discussion, based on the results.

Later that day, I paced down the feminine care aisle enveloped in pink and purple. Every box said a variation of the same thing: rapid results, early testing, digital response, immediate reading. Each of them claimed to be number one. I read every label. Back and forth, striding between brands and boxes and indecision. I couldn't choose. Eventually or reluctantly, I grabbed a box with two tests and headed for the register. I refused a bag, tucked the sensitive box into my coat pocket and went back home.

My roommate Ryan worked from home. As usual, he was camped out in his oversized easy chair in the middle of our living room with his computer on his lap. With a tight chest and a belly full of nerves, I plotted my route through the house to ensure minimal interaction. The only way to the bathroom was through the living room—no avoiding him. I entered the house clutching my coat tightly and removed my shoes, ensuring the long pink box in my pocket wasn't visible. I gingerly opened a cabinet. Without a sound, I grabbed an empty jar. I could hear Ryan on a conference call and I let out a sigh of relief. No need for idle chit-chat. I walked swiftly through the living room with a nod in his general direction and retreated to my bedroom. I tore open the tiny package and read the directions twice. I learned it's best to test early in the morning. With anxiety laboring my breath, I realized I hadn't had anything to eat or drink yet. There was no way I could wait until tomorrow.

I carefully opened my bedroom door to listen. Still on the phone. I tiptoed down the hall to our shared bathroom and closed the door. I peed into the clean jar and tore open the first stick. I dunked it into the jar and counted to five. I secured the cap back on the test and held my breath, waiting the recommended three minutes. Sitting on the bathroom floor, I re-read the directions. When it was time to read the results, I wasn't sure if there were two lines.

I carefully ripped open the other test, re-read the instructions, and tried again.

I got the same result—one faint line in front of a very solid line, maybe. I hurried out of the bathroom, doubling back to make sure I'd left no evidence, then dashed to my bedroom and closed the door behind me. I assumed extremely clear test results. Pregnant or not pregnant. This was inconclusive. I panicked.

Aside from prolonged period-like cramps, I felt normal. Considering how the last few months of unemployment had made me feel, maybe my pregnancy symptoms were hindered from the stress I felt. Then I second-guessed what pregnancy symptoms might be.

I turned to my computer for answers. All I found were pregnancy discussion forums. Desperate women seeking advice and moms of three responding with, "Congratulations! Baby on board!" I kept searching. I found a web page: *"Faint Positive Home Pregnancy Test: Am I Pregnant?"* It explained that the test measures the hCG hormone level. When the hormone is high, the dye in the test rushes to the first line, indicating a positive test.

I was pregnant.

Saying, "I love you," was still new for Dan and me. Our discussions of the future had no longevity. This would surely speed it up.

I shifted my internet search to find "pregnancy centers near me." I clicked through a few websites and scheduled an appointment for the next day at a clinic in town. Then I called Dan. He stayed calm. He kept reassuring me that we would figure it out. The next step was a doctor's appointment, and we would go from there.

I sat on the floor in the farthest corner of my bedroom, my legs pulled into my chest, whispering to Lisa over the phone. While she reassured me in my panic, I tried to find the details of my health insurance. I hadn't thought about it since I lost my job. I wondered if it was still active or if a pregnancy would be covered under a catastrophic plan. Lisa was surprisingly calm, even happy for me.

"Well, you'll know more tomorrow but I think this is great!" she said as she bounced her six-month-old in her lap. I wasn't so confident.

Shame

I was raised Catholic. The catechism teaches basic beliefs, how to live and how to pray, with certain social expectations. Go to mass every Sunday, tithe the church, confess, repent, do better, get married and consummate that promise with children. In that order. Misdeeds were made right with shotgun weddings and communal confessions, and we didn't really talk about it.

The first time I heard the phrase, "Catholic guilt," conflicted feelings had clouded my decision to leave Christmas dinner early. I was in my twenties and had made plans with my boyfriend. On my way out the door, with my uneasiness about leaving early written on my face, my aunt said, "Gotta love that Catholic guilt!" I resented the phrase. The idea that my guilt was a learned behavior, because of my faith, made me feel lousy. Faith was about personal reflection and acknowledging my shortcomings, learning compassion. It wasn't about obligation or constraint. I didn't understand the idea until I found myself in the waiting room of a pregnancy help center, wringing my hands at thirty years old, unmarried and pregnant.

I must have driven past the clinic dozens of times

and never noticed it. The office sat directly across the street from Planned Parenthood. I recognized the building because there were prayer groups camping outside every morning, rain or shine. Men and women, dressed for the weather, waving signs with graphic pictures of aborted fetuses, calling to end abortion. As I drove to my appointment, I wondered if a group of people stood waiting to greet me with their signs and shame. I looked around, taking inventory of my surroundings. Thankfully, I pulled into a driveway next to the unassuming building and parked in an empty lot. I took a deep breath; no prayer groups today.

The waiting room was empty except for me. A handful of chairs lined the wall and toddler toys filled a basket at the end of the row. The phone rang twice before I could check in. The receptionist spoke softly and with patience. When she was able, she greeted me with the same soft privacy and care. She took my name and told me to take a seat, that Eva would be with me in just a few minutes. I didn't know who Eva was and I could barely sit down. I managed to rest on the edge of my seat, sort of hovering between sitting and ready to pounce.

A petite woman with light brown and gray braids pulled back behind her neck appeared at the doorway near the reception desk. She introduced herself. Eva had the same air of patience and care as the receptionist. She ushered me down a short hallway and into a small, sterile exam room. She asked me several standard clinical questions. Sniveling between breathy answers, I turned the small, sealed cup she gave me over in my clammy hands. She offered a minute to collect myself and then gave directions to the bathroom. Every step, every move sent me closer to the uncertain reality of motherhood.

With a full cup and clean hands, I sat down across from her in an open waiting room lined with rigid black leather chairs with metal arms. I sat at the edge of the seat and rested my hands in my lap. While she used a small dropper to drip my sample onto a pregnancy test, she explained how it works. She placed the white test wrapper over the results while we waited the suggested three minutes. We were the only two people in the room. I looked around to see motherhood ads and "How To" brochures on the walls.

To fill the waiting, she asked me questions: Was I in a relationship? Was I safe? It surprised and depressed me to think that Dan could ever physically hurt me. I cried harder. My fear filled the room. I wondered how many women come to her in this way, full of dismay and uncertainty. How many women come from families and relationships that are unsupportive and unsafe. I had trouble explaining my apprehension, especially knowing what support I had with Dan.

What did I do for work?

Recently unemployed.

What was driving my fear?

How my family would react to this news.

Eva held my knee in one hand, as she lifted the wrapper from the test with the other. It revealed two pink lines.

Pregnant.

My guts flip-flopped where a baby would grow, was growing, and shame and worry filled me. I was supposed to have a plan, but my life suddenly felt directionless. I had no savings, a mediocre living situation, and nothing of my own to provide stability. I was independent, but only momentarily.

I would need to lean on Dan for complete financial support. I felt like a burden to him for this. I knew childbirth had a major price tag. The end of my unemployment loomed and my student loan deferment would end soon, too. These were all things we'd never discussed but would need to sort out. The only thing providing any comfort was knowing I had Dan by my side. We would work it out together.

Eva asked about my faith. I told her I identified as Catholic. She asked what I meant by that. I wasn't sure. I had never said it that way before, "I identify as Catholic." Until that moment I had believed in the Catechism of the Catholic Church but now I had made myself a walking contradiction to those ideals. This was the first time I felt searing guilt from unspoken rules. The anticipation of shame overshadowed the thrilling concept of becoming a mother. Instead of imagining who my child might be or preparing to welcome a baby into a space of love and care, I agonized over how we would share the news with our parents and grandparents who would expect marriage first.

The next step would be to schedule an ultrasound to find out how far along I was. Eva asked me again if I was safe at home and why I felt so upset. I tried to find the words but couldn't gather my thoughts. My family was loving and nurturing and faithful. They were always encouraging me, even when I felt aimless. A pregnancy was a dilemma that I hadn't seen them face before. I expected discomfort and disappointment when I broke the news.

Growing up, I understood that sex happened between husband and wife. That was it. We didn't discuss it any further. That worked for me because I was a rule-follower. I never tested limits, mostly because I was timid and unsure of myself. My boyfriends came and went because I intended to stay a virgin until I felt ready. I abstained partly because I was taught to wait until marriage, but also from fear of the unknown. What do you do with your hands? What if my body looked different? What if they had more experience and I was bad at it?

As I got older, I learned about sex by listening to friends at sleepovers. I acquired nicknames like "Prude," that frustrated and embarrassed me. But the risk of vulnerability was stronger than the peer pressure, so Prude I stayed. Sex seemed like the most unguarded action two people could share. I wasn't ready. Through high school and college, the idea of sharing something so intimate unnerved me. I had so much to sort out as a young adult: Who did I want to be? How would I make my mark on the world? Sex did not rank high on my list of priorities.

Catholics do not believe in birth control, so we didn't talk about it in my household aside from the one awkward week in eighth-grade health class. I declined to discuss birth control at annual OB GYN visits. I wasn't sexually active and without a medical need, it didn't feel like it applied to me.

As an adult, I learned how to track my cycle using a phone app and the advice of natural family planning.

Natural family planning is the method of tracking your cycle and abstaining until your fertile days. If you aren't trying to conceive, I suppose you would do the opposite.

Eva let me share my concerns until my eyes hurt from crying. I feared I wasn't a great example for a child when I felt so unaccomplished as an adult. I worried that my family would hold both me and my child at arm's length for the same reason. That was a heavy burden to carry and one I couldn't let go of until much later in my pregnancy.

We moved on to discuss prenatal care, with the clinic providing me with vitamin samples and a packet of information to go over with Dan. Her kindness created a sliver of light in a dark time. She showed me humanity when I anticipated the world turning against me. Eva was gentle and kind—she sat with me hand-in-hand while I let panic pour out of me. I didn't feel ready for a baby. I had lost my job. Dan and I had only recently started saying, "I love you." I never doubted his commitment, but we hadn't discussed having children until we were having one. Were we ready to be bonded for life?

I called Dan from the car to confirm a positive test. He acknowledged the information but carefully waited to follow my lead. He said he would be whatever I needed him to be. Partner, father, supporter, caregiver. I asked him to come with me to my follow-up appointment. I drove home and lay in bed until Dan finished work and came over.

A million questions rattled inside my head: How would we tell our parents? What would help them accept the news? What would my grandparents think? This isn't the shining example they would hope for me to set as the oldest granddaughter, how would this change the way they thought of me? Of my partner? The only control I had was in sharing the news. Everything else was their responsibility. But worry doesn't care about responsibility.

After a full week of anxiously weighing what-ifs, Dan and I parked outside the pregnancy center. Taking simultaneous deep breaths, we walked hand-in-hand into the clinic, ready for the follow-up ultrasound appointment. Immediately the environment felt different than last time. The all-female staff acted rigidly toward Dan as we entered the exam room. I was asked, for a third and fourth time, if I was comfortable having him in the room and if I consented to his presence during the examination.

Dry eyed but filled with uneasiness, I clambered up onto the table. I searched for a way to ease the tension but stayed quiet. The technician explained each step before she began the exam, checking my comfort level every few minutes. The room was quiet except for the crinkle of the sheet beneath me each time I took a deep breath. The sonographer took a few measurements, calling out each one, revealing that I was six weeks along. She gave us a USB drive with images and a sound clip of the baby's heartbeat. The baby's heartbeat, I had yet to learn how sweet that sound would be. The appointment ended with the promise of a call from the doctor with follow-up details.

Dan grabbed my hand as we walked out. Both of us let out a deep exhale when we got into the car. We went home with a mountain of new information and not much to say. We were both still wrapping our heads around the overwhelming idea of becoming parents. It felt like a big undertaking and yet there was nothing to DO to prepare ourselves. He waited for me to take the lead on how to feel and I couldn't feel anything but apprehension until I told my parents.

We needed a plan.

We talked about getting married. We both wanted to, but not right away. A decision to be married now would be made simply to uphold my family's expectations. I knew I didn't want to make that decision under those circumstances. Dan wasn't raised Catholic, so he didn't share the anguish I did about pregnancy before marriage. He did see the grief it caused me. He remained level-headed and thoughtful. He found ways to begin planning, starting with our living situation and financial status. I would move in with him now and we would tell his roommates when I was around six months pregnant, counting on their rent while we sorted out our joint cost of living.

With a plan in hand, I called my mom in the middle of a weekday, knowing my dad would be at work. If I told her one-on-one, I could gauge her reaction and brace myself for his. My mom and I don't usually fuss with small talk. I call several times a day for specific things, such as: How do I remove grape juice stains? Do you have my birth certificate? When's Grandma's birthday?

This time, I didn't know where to start. I knew she could hear it in my voice, so I blurted out, "I have to tell you something. I am pregnant, about six weeks. I went to a clinic and they confirmed it with an ultrasound. Dan and I talked about it, and I will move in with him before the baby arrives. We will get married, but not right now."

She quieted.

I gave her an out.

"You don't have to say anything, I know it's a lot."

I heard a deep breath, then: "I didn't think... you were... doing... that?"

Another long pause, this time from me. "Well... I'm *thirty.*"

Despite my age, and having never discussed sex, I knew pregnancy before marriage equaled irresponsibility. Catholicism speaks of sexual immorality—the presence of a child in the womb outside of marriage as the result of sinning. "Born out of wedlock," a term I've heard my family use to describe other situations that mirrored my own. As Catholics, we're taught that living together before marriage is one kind of sin. Unwed pregnancy? That's its own scarlet letter, glowing brighter with my growing belly, colored by the shame cast down from those beliefs. A recent headline of a schoolteacher, unmarried and pregnant, fired from her job at a Catholic elementary school only elevated my agony.

Mom and I quickly moved on to the elephant in the room—telling my dad. I asked for advice on how to tell him, silently praying she would offer to do it herself. Without hesitation, she said she would talk to him after work. She thought that if she told him, he wouldn't say anything he didn't mean to my face. My heart sank. Though I was relieved that there would be no confrontation, she confirmed my fear that he would meet this news with disappointment or even anger.

My mom texted me later that night. "Give him a few days." She wasn't specific and I didn't ask for details. I thought this would bring relief, but it only brought dread while I waited to hear from him.

Dan was raised Christian but not Catholic. His older sister had recently had a baby with her boyfriend the year before. A beautiful baby boy that brought joy to every moment. I watched his family navigate any tension with patience and humor. We intended to tell his dad and stepmom in person, after we heard from my dad.

Dan and I had previously planned a trip to Tennessee to visit my dad's sister Aunt Michele, who had just had a baby. We would meet my cousin and visit Nashville. We left the day after I told my mom. We swore ourselves to secrecy until all our parents knew. It was Super Bowl Sunday and I somehow managed to evade all offers of a beer or cocktail without raising suspicion. Aunt Michele is my dad's youngest sibling. With a sixteen-year age gap between them, and just eleven years between me and Michele, she's always felt more like a sister than an aunt. It was nearly impossible to keep such a big secret from her, especially because she was beginning her own new life of motherhood and I had so many questions.

Dan and I did some sightseeing in Nashville. I welcomed the break—a few hours of relief from keeping the secret. Despite my constant anxiety, I did my best to enjoy our trip. Dan and I toured a botanical garden that afternoon. We spent the day outside without pressure from anyone else, knowing the next eight months would prepare us for a lifetime together.

Driving down I-40 my phone rang. It was the pregnancy clinic calling to review our ultrasound. Everything looked normal and I should follow up with my OB-GYN in a few weeks. A shred of relief, but overshadowed by the wait of hearing from my dad. Later that afternoon I felt my phone buzz. A missed call from my dad, followed by a text.

"Don't be a coward. Answer my call."

I could hear his matter-of-fact tone while reading his words, causing me to hold my breath. The alarm sitting in my belly shifted to my throat. I called him back immediately. Lost in the fear of letting him down, I don't remember most of the conversation. My mom was right, my dad needed a day to process the news. He took a second day to devise a plan for Dan and I. In a very hopeful tone, he told me we would announce our engagement to my grandparents. And in a few months, we would share my pregnancy. He wanted them to know we had intentions of committing our lives to each other before we shared the news of a baby. He thought the announcement might be more well-received that way. I knew he was right. But it also meant bending the truth to our entire family, and for how long? He didn't sound mad. He wasn't upset with me. He didn't ask to speak sternly to Dan. Despite how uncomfortable his plan made me feel, I agreed with him. I couldn't bear to disappoint him further by objecting.

With two small words, "I'm pregnant," my entire life was altered. I had become someone else to my parents.

It felt as though I was no longer an independent, agreeable young lady. I became an embarrassing secret needing a cover-up. Dan and I headed home from Nashville without sharing our news.

I spent a few days building up the courage to call my mom again. I told her how important it was to Dan and me to get married for the right reasons. I wanted to go through the formal motions in the Catholic church with marriage and family preparation courses. I wanted our child to be baptized. I repeated that Dan and I intended to get married, but not before our baby arrived. I told her I was uncomfortable faking a wedding that had no date.

My dad was adamant, wedding first. My mom agreed to talk to him about it again. It hurt deeply that after thirty years of abiding by every rule, I was reduced to the one thing I did in the wrong order. It hurt that they took a position of damage control rather than celebration. During the weeks I was unable to share our news, I was robbed of any joy. Had we said all the unspoken things between us, I am certain a lot of anguish would have dissolved sooner.

My dad told my grandparents, his parents, about our non-existent engagement. They were thrilled. He asked them not to say anything—that it was my wish to tell everyone individually. Another lie hammering down another layer of anxious waiting. My grandmother texted me, begging me to tell my aunts so we could all share in the news together. My grandparents. The patriarch and matriarch of our family. Along with my own parents, their authority and influence are strong and lasting. I spent thirty years seeking their approval out of respect. I wanted to make them proud. I called my mom crying, a final plea, begging her to help me tell the truth. I told her that the lying hurt more than their disappointment would.

Finally, my dad told them the truth, which also meant he had accepted the truth. That was important to me. I asked how they took it. My mom said they simply asked if I was okay and said they would pray for me. A window of relief opened. I could tell the rest of my family. Telling aunts, uncles and cousins carried less anxiety. They had a less authoritative, more supportive role in my life.

I told Michele first. When she lit up with excitement, it took me by surprise. No one else in my family had reacted that way! She asked if we were happy.

She asked if we were happy.

Michele had gone through a divorce a few years before. I didn't know the extent of her struggle until I shared my own. Knowing the religious views of our family and having her own adversity with the pressure of Catholicism, she asked if my parents were on board. I explained the complicated tangle we were in. She gave me comfort and assured me our family would come around.

"If they can get over divorce, they can surely get through this."

Then she skipped back to the excitement and added her sister, my aunt Patrice, to the call. They shared their stories of parenting and newborns, reminiscing on their own new mom experiences. I sat on my bed hanging on every breath of enthusiasm from my aunts as I looked down at my growing belly. The excitement was late, but here it was. And it was vibrant! I looked around the attic bedroom I now shared with Dan and I felt like everything would be okay. We tossed around baby name ideas, and we cried together in anticipation. It was the first time I was given permission to feel excitement for my pregnancy. No one had asked any questions beyond: Will you get married? When?

...

We were ready to let Dan's parents in on our news. We went to dinner at his dad's house. Dan is a lot like his dad, easy-going, kind and unassuming. While we drove over to their house, I kept asking Dan for his plan—how would he tell them, when would he tell them. I'd only met them a few times and I was nervous.

Bill and Martha (Dan's dad and stepmom) had welcomed their first grandson the year before. We witnessed their acceptance through that first experience. Dan held no reservations about what their response to our news would be.

He shrugged.

"I don't know. I'll just tell them."

Halfway through dinner, Dan told them we would be welcoming a baby in the fall. Bill's face lit up in surprise. "Well, how about that," he said, grinning from ear to ear.

Always polite, Martha laughed and clapped her hands together, almost in relief. She told Dan she had been worried I would move back to Detroit. Dan was dragging his feet. She was glad this meant I would be sticking around.

Met with enthusiasm again, I felt a heavy weight lifting.

...

The arrival of spring meant Easter Sunday and the first family gathering since our news had been shared. I was fifteen weeks along and barely showing. I wore a conservative, A-line skirt, belted above my waist. It hid my bump in case I made anyone uncomfortable. I wasn't sure how I would be received and I didn't want to flaunt my growing belly if they weren't ready to process it. It's still hard for me to consider that my mere presence, and the baby inside my body, may have been offensive. Dan and I were still adjusting to our shock and surprise, so concealing my belly allowed us more private time to settle in. Dan remained a supportive listener. He felt that my issues with my family were something I would resolve, and they had less to do with him and more to do with an outdated set of rules.

I walked into my aunt and uncle's house. Everyone greeted us as usual with warm smiles and gentle hugs. A happy Easter, indeed. My grandmother gave me a long embrace. She said she had a prayer card in the car she would like to give me. I followed her back outside. Waiting barefoot like a child on the lowest porch step, I watched her walk back from the car. I am a few inches taller than her on level ground. In this instance, standing a step above, I towered over her. She handed me a large yellow envelope, inside was a Father Solanus prayer. She gently pulled it out for me to read.

"Life is to live and life is to give and talents are used for good if you choose. Do not pray for easy lives; pray to be strong. Do not pray for tasks equal to your powers. Pray for powers equal to your tasks, then the doing of your work shall be no miracle, but you shall be a miracle. Every day you shall wonder at yourself, at the richness of life, which has come to you by the grace of God."

Then she took both of my hands into hers and sincerely thanked me for not having an abortion.

When I heard her say the word, "abortion," I felt my whole body shrink in size. I had never felt so small. The thought of ending my pregnancy had never once crossed my mind. Though the sentiment was supportive, and her intentions good, I felt devastated. I resisted the urge to burst into tears. It would take me more than a year to figure out why that comment hurt me so much.

I think there's a misconception that abortion is often a matter of convenience. To think I might choose to abort my unborn, simply because I wasn't married, hurt. My parents raised me to be independent. My dad taught me how to change my own oil and brake pads, to shoot free throws in the driveway after a game, to have a firm handshake and never back down in an argument. But I was still his little girl. Perhaps my being pregnant and unmarried may have felt to him like I didn't have a safety net and he wanted to protect me. Though the timing wasn't ideal, we had no doubts about keeping our child. Dan and I were confident in our partnership and in our ability to work together in life and now in parenthood. Though we weren't quite prepared for the surprise, we were willing to rise to the task together.

Insurance

Just before our Easter family visit, I moved out of my rental and into Dan's house, one he'd bought five years ago with a HUD grant before the economy recovered. He paid the fifteen-year, fixed mortgage by renting out the bedrooms. Initially, we told all four roommates I moved in as a cost-saving measure while I continued my job search. Eventually, we held a house meeting to share the news of our pending addition and politely ask his roommates to find new living arrangements. They shared their excitement for us and were able to find new apartments with ease.

Dan and I began turning his house into our home. We started by deep cleaning and painting each room. We picked the smallest bedroom on the second floor and put a nursery together. We decided not to learn the baby's sex until they were born and kept the space free of blue and pink. We agreed on a soft green for the walls and an oatmeal white for the trim. I searched high and low for the perfect gray and white shag rug. My grandparents sent us a beautiful white crib that I put together while Dan was at work. I ordered white knit curtains with gray branches growing from the bottom up. We started collecting books to add to the gray bookshelf my aunt and uncle sent us. The initial discomfort of shock and disappointment had thawed. Our families were accepting and excited to share in the growth of our family.

Dan and I settled into a routine. He went to work each day from a local coffee shop with proper WIFI, while I applied for jobs and saved references for unemployment, taking naps in between to escape my anxiety. My pants no longer came together at my belly, so I borrowed from a close friend. She gave me a giant bag full of dresses, shorts, pants, and shirts. I wore a gray and black striped T-shirt dress all summer long. My body changed rapidly, encouraging friends and family to ask how I was feeling. Despite the insatiable need for fresh fruits and vegetables, I had constant heartburn, no matter what I ate. Because I was still unemployed, I wasn't sure if my insurance had lapsed. Each month, I requested my payment for unemployment. I filled out the paperwork to prove I was applying for jobs, provided my debt-to-income ratio, filled out a Medicaid application, then verified my pregnancy to make sure the cost of childbirth would be covered. Each hoop required me to prove my worth. Several dozen phone calls, often being put on lengthy holds, and mailing and faxing forms all led to weeks of waiting. I continued applying for jobs, half-heartedly knowing they would take one look at me and move on to the next candidate. Because Dan and I weren't married, I couldn't be added to his private insurance plan.

Finally, after three months, I was granted minimal coverage. Shadowed by shame, again, I was provided with a list of doctors that accepted Medicaid. These programs, built for people who need them—and I needed them—made me feel unworthy. I felt marginalized by everyone I called during the approval process, as if somehow, I was a criminal, stealing their services. I told myself this was temporary. I felt the need to justify my situation and my character. Government-funded insurance was created for people in a tight financial spot. I was resentful that needing this program reflected my value. I had paid into Medicaid my entire adult life. Yet, when I needed help the most, I felt the deepest shame in asking for it.

...

A series of parking ramps and ticket stamps and a new doctor's office. With no Eva to hold my hand, I felt nervous. This was my first appointment since the pregnancy confirmation and a six-week ultrasound at the clinic. Because of all the paperwork and waiting, I was now twenty-eight weeks along.

I told Dan he didn't need to come with me. We weren't scheduled for an ultrasound so there was no need for his company. The waiting room was average—an office with too many bright lights and large windows looking out over the expressway. Flanked by reception desks and a coffee counter, a dozen pregnant women waited in the center of the room. Some stood with their partners, some entertained their young children with iPads and earbuds. I sat down and kept my gaze at my feet, expecting my name to be called. The occasional bing of the elevator kept me on high alert.

The office door swung open and a nurse called my name. I followed her to a scale, surrounded by polite nurses buzzing about their daily tasks.

In soft pink scrubs, the nurse stood about two inches taller than me and had brown hair pulled back in a bun at the nape of her neck.

"OK, you can step off the scale," she said, writing furiously in my chart. "Late to seek care," she cited out loud and continued writing as though irresponsible ignorance, and not paperwork delays, had kept me from looking after my baby. Over the file in her hands, she looked down her nose at me to ask for a reason. I stumbled through a brief explanation of unemployment and insurance applications, noting my check-up at the pregnancy clinic. I focused my gaze back to my shoes.

With a courteous look, I was ushered into a clinic room. A second nurse, tapping on her laptop, also noted my gestation and lateness to seek care before checking my blood pressure and gathering my medical history. She gave me a gown and left me to wait for the doctor. I looked around the room. A framed certificate on the wall told me the OB was a graduate of the University of Detroit Mercy. As I undressed, I thought, "A Detroiter— at least we have something in common."

Finally, the doctor came into the room and introduced himself. Smartly dressed, he looked extremely tall in such a small room, with wire-framed glasses and a white lab coat. His introduction felt formal. I mentioned his certificate on the wall to break the ice, sharing that my paternal grandparents were also alumni. He nodded and moved right into my medical history, noting that growth ultrasound usually occurs around twenty weeks. He performed a routine OB-GYN exam and discussed any history of pregnancy, miscarriage or abortion. The conversation was short because no such history existed. He also pointed out that I was eight weeks behind for the ultrasound. We scheduled my next appointment, in two weeks' time, to include an ultrasound at thirty weeks gestation.

I thought after the appointment I'd feel better—more confident, less anxious. But I felt unsettled with the constant reminder of delayed prenatal care. I told everyone that the baby and I were healthy, lying about how frequent my check-ups had been, promising to share a photo after my next appointment. I still kept so much to myself—my defeat from losing my job, my worry over so urgently needing the financial support of Dan, my blunder with changing insurance and embarrassment in needing Medicaid. It felt like it was my job to manage others' perceptions of me. I didn't want my family or friends to think less of me for having these other problems, so I kept the details to myself, thinking less information would mean fewer judgments. I hadn't considered that this tactic also prevented anyone from helping me.

PART II

Diagnosis

Dan came with me to my next appointment. This was the part where the hard moments would melt away and we would see our baby. Joy and love and anticipation would take over! Our future would become more focused, more real. We were going to become parents together. Knowing the route to the office, I led Dan through the parking ramp and up the elevator.

The ultrasound technician guided us to an identical room like last time, this time with an ultrasound machine. She turned down the lights and got straight to work. She measured the fluid around the baby, then moved on to the kidneys, the heart. She explained that because I was farther along than twenty weeks, it was more difficult to view all the baby's anatomy. She called another technician in to help. They pointed to the screen and muttered to one another about outflow tracts. She mentioned having a more in-depth scan because she was having trouble viewing the baby's heart. She stopped abruptly and stepped out to get the doctor. Dan and I looked at each other with confusion. Unsure if we should worry, we waited.

The technician returned with the doctor, and they

had the same discussion. He explained that a few parts of the heart, because of size, were hard to see this far along in pregnancy. He referred us to a Maternal-Fetal Medical (MFM) specialist for a fetal echocardiogram with, "nothing to worry about."

Dan and I spent a long weekend with my extended family in Frankfurt, Michigan, to celebrate my grand-parent's 60th wedding anniversary. The vacation soft-ened the rawness I felt after so much unspoken unrest between me, my parents and grandparents. I was preg-nant and we were all okay.

Dan and I left our family vacation a day early to come home for the fetal echocardiogram. We brushed off any prying inquiries by saying the doctor's office was booked and unable to reschedule, keeping the nature of the ap-pointment to ourselves. After all, it could be nothing. We gave ourselves plenty of time in the morning to arrive at our appointment early. It marked our first experience finding our way through the parking ramps for the hos-pital downtown, in a maze of offices I had never seen before; I didn't want to be late.

This waiting room was split in two—one side for adults and the other for children. The children's side had a huge TV playing fast-talking cartoons. Bright colors and miles of sound flew around the room, jarring at first, but a welcomed distraction as we waited.

Engaging all my sitting muscles, I sat tall in a chair made for two, elbow to elbow with Dan. Dan doesn't get nervous, but a combination of it being a more in-depth check and having him take the day off to be with me, made the appointment feel more serious. Just one other person sat on the adult side of the waiting room, reading a magazine, unfazed by the wildfire of cartoons zooming around in all directions. A nurse entered the waiting room from a doorway at the end of a long corridor. Walking toward us, she called my name. We followed her back to the area where she recorded my height and weight and took measurements of my belly. All standard steps I had experienced each prenatal visit. I realized I was holding my breath. I exhaled slowly as we followed her back to the exam room. Everything was gray and white and sterile.

The technician introduced herself and explained this appointment would unfold much like a normal ultrasound, but they would take more detailed images of the baby's heart for the specialist to review. She squeezed a snake of jelly onto my abdomen, warm and clear blue like hair gel. All three of us stayed silent. She clicked on her computer and focused on her monitor, slowly rolling the doppler wand over my big belly. No one spoke for a long time. The weight of this appointment and what it might mean hung heavy in the air. I kept trying to find something to talk about to dissolve the tension as Dan held my hand. My palms, matching Dan's, were cold and damp. I kept taking long, slow inhales but I couldn't shake the feeling that something was wrong.

I watched every move the sonographer made. She was polite and methodical in her preparation. I wanted her to remind me of my mother, lending me some type of comfort, but there was no maternal safety in her company. Her movements were slow and methodical, turning a dial and clicking, recording bits, and measuring pockets of gray matter on her monitor. Sometimes we heard sounds of the baby's heartbeat, recorded for the doctor to review. But she never discussed any of the steps she was expertly navigating.

I checked the clock over the door. She'd been scanning my belly for nearly an hour. I wondered about the average length of an appointment like this. What if there was something to worry about? A rush of panic shivered through me. I thought about asking to use the bathroom but told myself to wait a few minutes more. The appointment should be over soon. I noticed that each time the sonographer moved the ultrasound wand, she touched her left hand to her face. She rested the inside of her index, middle, and ring finger over her mouth as she furrowed her brow. I watched her repeat this half a dozen times. I told myself to wait for the doctor but the next time she brought her hand to her face, I could no longer hold back the worry. My feelings spilled out in every direction with no way to pull them back in.

"I'm so scared," I cried out uncontrollably. "I'm so scared."

The ultrasound technician gave me a sincere and sympathetic look. She rested her hand on my shoulder and said, "Oh, it's going to be okay. It looks like there may be an issue with the outflow tracts. I'll get the doctor."

She handed me a box of thin hospital tissues and swiftly left the room. Mine and Dan's feelings of helplessness were palpable. Before we had the chance to talk to each other, a different nurse entered the room. I grabbed a handful of scratchy tissues and she escorted us to the consultation space. Another clinical room, nearly identical to the last, but larger in size. In place of an exam table and sonogram computer, there was a couch. We set our coats down and sat together, staring at the door in silence.

When the doctor entered the room, I thought we'd both pounce on him. He was stout and solid with a short beard and kind eyes. Dr. Columbo sat down and introduced himself. I could feel his empathy feeding my dread. Dr. Columbo explained the anatomy of the heart and how our baby's heart had all the correct parts, but the plumbing was wrong. He went on to say our baby had Transposition of the Great Arteries (TGA) and Double Outlet Right Ventricle (DORV), which meant the two main arteries of the heart (aorta and pulmonary valve) were switched and led into the same ventricle, instead of opposite ventricles. Our baby also had some thickening heart tissue outside of his pulmonary valve. All of this hinders the body's ability to pump oxygen-rich blood to parts of the body. To compensate for that, the baby has developed a Ventricular Septal Defect (VSD), which is a hole between the ventricles, to encourage more blood circulation, allowing an outlet for oxygen-rich blood to get to the body.

Dan and I were stunned. Miles of brand-new information came rushing at us from every direction. It felt like the doctor had switched languages while my brain frantically took notes to keep up. He moved on to the specifics. There would be no need for any emergency delivery but once the baby was born, they would need to operate within the first week of life, which meant post-operative recovery in the pediatric intensive care unit

(PICU). Dr. Columbo assured us that, although what he'd just said sounded abnormal for us, they saw these types of heart defects frequently. He reiterated that our baby was safest inside my body, then he asked if we had questions. Bleary-eyed, overwhelmed, and unable to comprehend what he had just told us, it would be weeks before I could even formulate questions. We scheduled a follow-up appointment to meet the pediatric cardiologist and drove home.

I called my mom, and then Lisa, when we got home. I told them, as best as I could, what the doctor had said. They both shared similar opinions, it could be fixed, just one surgery, maybe it won't be so bad. Open heart surgery on my infant didn't seem like a minor repair. Numb to their idealism, I hurried off the phone and sat on our bed. Dan ended a call with his dad, and we laid in bed, in the middle of the day, for a nap, with nothing to do but wait.

We met the cardiologist a week later. More petite than I expected, she greeted us warmly.

"Hi, I'm Dr. Heather Sowinski," she said. "I know you met with Dr. Columbo and he went over the baby's diagnosis with you. I want you to know this isn't something you've caused."

The sentiment rang out in my head as I considered everything I may have done wrong. Was it the second whiskey I had on New Year's Eve before I knew I was pregnant? Or when I went to the nail salon in my second trimester? The staff always wore masks. I should have, too. The nail tech smudged two nails and had to start over, extending the appointment. I remember wanting to tell him never mind so I could sprint from his chair to my car, but I was afraid of being rude.

Was it the first few weeks without prenatal vitamins?

Was it the all-consuming anxiety I could never keep away?

I waved those thoughts away and let her words sink in.

"This is nothing you've done," she said. "You didn't cause this, and you could not have prevented it." She repeatedly looked at us with such care and concern, like old friends, like we hadn't just met. Like she wouldn't have to make hard decisions to safeguard the wellbeing of my unborn child.

"Nice to meet you," I muttered as I studied her face. She went over the diagnosis again—transposition of the Great Arteries, double outlet right, arterial switch operation. A few of the words flying around the room began to feel familiar. She explained our baby would be monitored at birth in the Neonatal Intensive Care Unit (NICU). Once we determined a surgical date, we would be monitored in the Pediatric Intensive Care Unit for post-operative recovery. New words, all foreign. She introduced us to the staff and gave us a tour of both ICU floors. I couldn't tell the hallway from the elevator. I promised myself I'd remember it when I needed to. We landed back at the cardiology reception to make a follow-up appointment with her and my OB to discuss delivery.

***

On an ordinary day, around thirty-six weeks pregnant, Dan was upstairs getting dressed while I stood in our orange kitchen at our breakfast table. I could feel our baby wiggling around in my belly. I remembered the doctor saying the baby was safest with me. I thought about how the minute he was born I would be unable to protect him or keep him safe. I sat down and put my hands over the spot where I felt the most movement. Dan came running, unsure if my howls were joy or sorrow, as my tears filled our kitchen. We had hurdled over so much and finally arrived at a place of excitement, only for it to be overshadowed by a complicated medical diagnosis and impending surgery. I felt conflicted. I wanted to meet my child, but I also wanted to keep them safe. Knowing that I couldn't do both terrified me.

Faith

I was raised Catholic. We believe in one God, maker of Heaven and Earth. We believe in Jesus Christ, begotten-not made, incarnate by the Holy Spirit. He became man, was crucified and died for our sins. We believe he rose again and ascended into Heaven. We believe in the communion of saints, the forgiveness of sins, the resurrection of the body, and life everlasting, Amen.

As a rule follower, the consequences of these ideals never applied to me. I joined the youth group in middle school and began teaching catechism in high school. When I moved away for college, I joined a local parish and attended weekly mass on my own. I observed holy days and prayed the rosary while driving to work. I was desperate for a deeper understanding of the world around me. I used prayer to talk me through the tough stuff in college, providing clarity and purpose. Time alone, with my mind and my heart, helped me through the heartache of unexpected loss. It helped me navigate growing up.

Prayer helped, until it didn't.

When I learned I was pregnant, I worried about what everyone else would think. I thought my faith would bring me comfort when I needed compassion. Unspoken social expectations had a major hold on my self-worth. Though no one said a word, I felt disparaged by my faith family. I tried leaning into prayer but praying to God felt like begging. It stunk of desperation and it elevated my torment. As a sinner, I was supposed to ask for forgiveness, but I wasn't sorry. How could I be both a good Catholic and a good mother if I wasn't seeking redemption?

I turned to the Blessed Solanus Casey, a name I knew from church. My family attended mass at St. Bonaventure Chapel, his resting place, in Detroit. Solanus was a Capuchin monk so moved by the Holy Spirit that he wanted to share it with everyone he met. Not a bright scholar, he was denied entry into the priesthood several times. He was finally admitted under strict guidelines that he wouldn't hear formal confessions. He became the Doorkeeper of Detroit, providing comfort and a listening ear to anyone who needed it. He died in 1957. There are photographs of Solanus on streets I've walked, in chapels I've attended. He felt more approachable than God. I leaned on him as a prayer editor.

I shared my unfiltered mournings and weepings, and he refined them. I thought if he felt moved, he might put in a good word for me and leave out the desperate parts.

Prayer is less about the result and more about the action of reflection. I could see that in my contemplations with Blessed Solanus, I felt an unfettering relief from my despair, if only momentarily, building my resilience. He wasn't the one with all-knowing power. As a confidante, a friend, he listened without judgment. I pleaded for answers from the doorkeeper, searching for a kind of validation I couldn't name, hoping time and prayer would make me feel less guilty and more prepared for motherhood.

Birthday

At a final visit with my OB-GYN at thirty-eight weeks, I brought Dan to help advocate that induction would not be necessary. Showing no sign of labor, my body wasn't ready. I needed more time. The doctor heard little of what I wanted, and insisted we had no choice. It's hard to talk to the people in charge when they aren't willing to listen. Despite my concerns, he scheduled an induction for the following week.

The night of my induction, the weather was unseasonably warm for September. Humid air hung heavy around us with little relief after sunset. We ordered a vegetarian pizza from our favorite local shop for dinner, Martha's Vineyard. They called it, "The Mike," and toppings were a surprise based on what they had fresh and in season. Ours came with arugula, watermelon radishes, and a balsamic reduction atop a thin, warm flatbread—unusual and delicious. My last meal before meeting our baby. I drank a cherry Coke and tried not to think about what the next twenty-four hours might bring. Packing my bag was simple, just a few comforts for me—nursing bras, my own blanket, a toothbrush and hair ties, and a few items for the baby—an outfit or two, a pacifier, a Blessed Solanus prayer relic. The hospital would provide anything else we needed.

Night had fallen by the time we got into the car to head to the hospital. It started to rain as we turned up the brick-paved hill to the maternity entrance. Dan dropped me at the roundabout at 9 p.m., right on time. I waited in the lobby while he parked. I nodded to the security guard while I stood just inside the revolving door. The first-floor lobby had two-story ceilings with a giant Dale Chihuly chandelier. Colorful snakes of glass coiling out in all directions made the space feel bright and happy, a stark contrast to the sticky weather, and my nervous fear. I kept reminding myself to focus on the next steps: wait for Dan, check-in, get to a hospital room. Even though I felt petrified, waiting for Dan was easy enough, walking to the check-in desk seemed manageable. This laser focus, on one menial task after another, kept me from falling into desperate hysteria.

It took two hours to settle into the room overlooking a towering cement building. We drew the shade. My hospital gown came with two IVs, one for fluids and the other for medications to induce contractions. And that was it. Nurses checked on me throughout the night. The medication caused uncomfortable cramping and insomnia, but made little progress toward active labor and delivery. Dan tried to get comfortable. He folded blankets and a crunchy hospital pillow into a makeshift bed on the pull-out couch, a glorified cot. With the shade drawn, unable to tell the day from the night, we tried to rest without much success.

The morning brought a shift change and a series of eager, fresh-faced nurses encouraging me to move around. Dan held me around the waist while I pushed the IV pole, hoping laps through the halls of labor and delivery may stimulate the natural rhythm of my body. We whispered encouragement to our unborn baby while we walked. My doctor stopped by. Disappointed in the lacking progress made overnight, he decided to break my water. My fear intensified with the cramping and the waiting. The only way out of this was through it. Overwhelmed and afraid of how much endurance childbirth would require, while fretting about the unknown wellness of my child—I asked for an epidural.

The anesthesiologist came to our room with his own nursing team. They helped me sit on the edge of the bed and lean forward with my head toward my knees. I couldn't see a single thing they were doing. I heard sounds of packages tearing, plastic syringes clicking together. A strong sterile smell of rubbing alcohol and adhesive rose to meet me while I prayed for them to finish, to provide some relief. They left as quickly as they had arrived so I could rest. The nursing team kept asking what I'd like to do, but I never had a proper answer. I grew more panicked as things progressed—I needed someone else to take charge.

A third shift change brought a new energy of nurses, including Carla. She could read my uncertainty and took over instantly. She moved like clockwork, shifting my body into one position, watching the monitors, reading the progress, and then moving me again. Her assertiveness allowed me momentary relief, freedom from decision-making. Our fast friendship lessened the blow when she told me that despite our best efforts, waiting had become dangerous for our unborn baby. Labor was putting stress on our baby's heart. I needed a Cesarean. Carla gently placed the oxygen mask over my face as I hyperventilated. My first panic attack. Dan held my hand while trying to swallow his own shock and fear. A flurry of medical staff surrounded us, preparing to transport me to an operating room. I looked at Dan and repeated, "I don't want this. I don't want this."

Throughout our birthing class, months before, the instructor encouraged us to create a birth plan to include who we wanted in the room, what types of medication we would allow, if we chose cord blood banking or vitamin K. A long list. I didn't make a birthing plan. I knew anything I planned would not consider the specific situation we were in. There would constantly be more information available that would need considering before making the best decision for the wellness of our baby. The only thing I wanted was to have my baby naturally. And now, that wasn't going to happen. Devastation filled me.

I pulled at the oxygen mask, "I don't want this!" I pleaded to Dan.

No one else heard me, or they weren't listening, except Dan, but he felt helpless, too. My begging scared him. We were coming to the end of my ability to keep our baby safe. The unknown of what would happen next was like a deep black hole we were being propelled toward, against our will. I felt terrified. Would they take my baby away? Would our baby die before we gave them a name?

Nurse Carla helped everything move swiftly. My bed rolled from the maternity ward to the delivery room with ease. Women filled the delivery room—including a team of nurses preparing instruments and linens, doctors tending to my medications, IVs, and surgical needs, and a NICU team eagerly awaiting the baby's arrival. Crowded. Dan dressed quickly in his scrubs and cap while they strapped my arms to the table. Splayed out, my body T-shaped. Dan tucked in over my left shoulder, unable to hold my hand. I could feel his presence, but I couldn't see him.

The anesthesiologist hovered over me, checking in. I felt an increased sharpness in my shoulders, and she administered medication for what she called, "residual pain." A nurse put a small tray near my cheek which I put to quick use by vomiting out my fears. Things moved fast. The surgeon asked if Dan wanted to call out our baby's gender.

"I... I don't want to see anything gross," he blurted out.

Between snivels and spit-ups, I called out to Carla. Moments later she hollered, "Are you ready? It's a baby boy!"

"Is he okay?" I kept repeating.

I closed my eyes, desperate to hear his voice. With his first cry came a flood of relief. After measurements, a quick clean-up, and a swaddle, the NICU team brought our baby boy close to my head. The nurses all congratulated us and cooed over such a sweet bundle. They did their best to get him into my line of sight. I couldn't hold him or smell him or take him in. I could barely see him, but I knew he was breathing on his own. I also knew he needed to leave me to be given his best chance. I kept assuring Dan that despite the constant flow of tears and vomit, I felt okay, and that he could go with our baby. Reluctantly, he followed our son into the NICU while the surgical team stapled me back together.

I laid there alone in a room full of people without the slightest idea of what came next.

From start to finish, the surgery had taken 30 minutes. They wheeled me into a recovery room with my entire body involuntarily and uncontrollably shaking. Nurse Carla came to my rescue again, this time armed with a breast pump and bottles. She hooked me up to the pump and explained that the shaking came from all the adrenaline in my body, assuring me it would go away on its own within hours. Additionally, I needed to be monitored until the anesthesia wore off to confirm a stable blood pressure and to rule out any hemorrhaging before I could reunite with my baby.

Several hours had passed since I had caught a glimpse of him. Finally, Carla expertly guided my hospital bed through a labyrinth of hallways to the Children's Hospital NICU. They were able to unlatch the double door to fit my hospital bed into the room where a little boy lay.

My son.

By now, it was the middle of the night/early morning. I could see Dan in the dimly lit room, eager and relieved for my arrival. He turned to me and delivered our son into my arms. This memory is vivid, but no words can possibly carry its power. He came wrapped tightly in a white receiving blanket with a blue and pink stripe down the middle. He had three small cords stuck to his chest and an intimidating IV in his forehead. Right away I could tell he had my nose, but his eyes were all Dan.

I held my baby.

And I wept.

We were both okay.

It was a great relief to see my baby boy swaddled and warm like all the other newborns, breathing on his own. I cannot recall what time it was, or how long we spent together. Eventually, fatigue won out and they wheeled me to a new room on the maternity ward while our son had to remain in observation in the NICU. Dan followed behind and tried to recount each moment I had missed. My eyes stung, swollen from crying. While listening to Dan recount the time I had missed, I realized I still couldn't feel my lower body. We got to our room and settled in to rest. Pulling swaddle blankets from our packed bag, I tucked a few inside the top of my hospital gown in the hopes that my scent would bring comfort to our son. In the moment, their newness and softness brought comfort to me. We arranged the elevation of my bed to a comfortable position. I tried to rest, waking every few hours for medication. They assured me our baby would sleep while I slept, and I could return in a few hours.

I don't recall falling asleep, but I must have drifted off once we turned out the lights. I woke to the nurse checking my vitals and providing pain medication. She was noiseless, but the opening of the door revealed the fluorescent hallway and jolted us from dreamland to reality.

I was a mom.

Dan was a dad.

We were a family, and our baby was in intensive care.

The nurse left as quietly as she had come.

Dan and I made a slow start to our day. With his help, I sat up and swung my legs over the side of the bed in preparation to stand, a very intimidating task when your belly is stapled shut. Desperate not to engage my abdomen, I used my arms to slide my butt to the end of the bed until I felt my feet hit the floor. I leaned forward, bending at my waist until my feet were fully supporting my body. I wanted to move quickly, to rush back to our baby and memorize his face, but I could barely get out of bed. Slowly, I straightened my back to sit up tall.

In my tan hospital socks covered with little white gripping pads, I slowly raised one foot, moving it a few inches in front of the other. I repeated this action with the other foot, sluggishly shuffling forward until I reached the threshold of the bathroom. Dan milled around the room, tidying blankets and gathering supplies. I took a moment and stood in front of the mirror. My hair looked like a tangled mess. My eyes were still a tender pink and swollen from crying. My forearms were already bruised blue and purple from IVs and blood draws. I gently raised the bottom of my hospital gown, loosely tied around one shoulder. I inched it up in the palms of my hands. Without bending, I took inventory of my swollen belly, smaller than yesterday and lined with a neat row of silver staples complemented by a white gauze bandage. They wouldn't let me shower until they removed the staples. Later in the evening, the doctor arrived to do just that. She assured me I wouldn't feel anything as the nerves in this area were severed during surgery. It would likely take the better part of the year for those nerves to heal. She was right—I felt a little pressure and a gentle tug with each staple, but no pain. She fastened a few adhesive bandages over the wound and told me not to saturate or scrub them in the shower.

I made my meager shuffle back to the bathroom for a rinse. I stood with my back in the hot water, washing my hair. It felt good to let the hot water fall around me, rinsing away bits of trauma. I was able to dress myself in hospital attire and comb my hair while Dan stepped into the hall to request a wheelchair, eager to see his baby while honoring my needs at the same time. He padded the chair with pillows and a blanket. He tucked the diaper bag over his shoulder while I lowered my battered body into the chair.

We rolled into an elevator, then to the ramp connecting the adult hospital to the children's hospital. We stopped at their front desk facing a three-story wall of white paneled glass. Each section, filled with water, lights up a different color as bubbles drift up and down. It was soothing and mesmerizing. The receptionist created our long-term parent badges with a parking pass and gave us directions to the NICU.

Another elevator brought us to the sixth floor and another desk with a smiling receptionist to greet us. We filled out a few forms and provided information on our baby. She gave us a generous donation of baby blankets and hats. We thanked her and made our way to the double doors. Dan scanned his badge and the doors swung open to reveal a rounded corridor of little apartments, each door adorned with baby names and photos, except ours. Our baby still didn't have a name.

Our child lay there quietly resting, breathing, and pulsing on his own. I hadn't allowed myself to imagine this moment. I wasn't sure how he would arrive, or how urgent his needs would be. I had been in survival mode for so long, I hadn't thought about how I would get to know my son. There he slept in his isolette—a small hospital bed made specifically for an infant. It's a clear, plexiglass rectangle with four hinged sides. The two longer sides each have a pair of round openings, allowing hands to reach in to touch or monitor the baby and check vitals, without disturbing. All the gadgets were intimidating at first, but they became a comfort after learning what service each part provided. To the right of the door was a long countertop with a sink, surrounded by cabinets above and below. The nurse told us our cardiologist had already been by, but would return later to see us.

We entered his dark room. The lights were off, except for a small overhead glow at the sink and the colorful monitors blinking rates and numbers. The isolette stood tall across the room. The nurse's rolling desk was stationed between the isolette and sliding door, complete with a computer and barcode scanner on top of a locked cabinet, home to medical dressings and medications.

To the left of the isolette was a small countertop and cabinet for parents, two reclining chairs, and a side table. It all provided a comfortable space to learn the needs of our baby and we took full advantage. Dan and I spent the day going back and forth between visiting our son and taking naps in our room in the maternity ward. We became experts in navigating the IV line and heart monitor cords to change diapers. Dan mastered maneu-. vering me around the hospital in a wheelchair. I learned to use the breast pump and how to feed my newborn.

Our cardiologist met us that afternoon. She confirmed that the diagnosis was the same—TGA, DORV with a VSD, and pulmonary stenosis. I looked at our tiny, sleeping infant swaddled in a muslin blanket. An IV pierced the scalp above his right eye, hindering any view of his perfectly round face—a glaring reminder of the seriousness that came next. He was stable. They would keep him in the NICU for a full week to monitor his oxygen saturations and blood levels. The cardiologist gave us a little hope by sharing that he might be able to come home before surgery. It caught us off guard. Bringing him home before surgery was something we had never considered. Much like the rest of this experience, I refused to imagine this possibility until it was real.

We spent several days oscillating between caring for our newborn son and getting rest. He hadn't needed any additional medical support, so we were left alone to marvel at our little baby most of the day. We spent afternoons taking turns holding our baby and watching him sleep, exchanging name suggestions, determined to find the perfect one. A name was a great responsibility.

He would carry this badge for the rest of his life. I kept a running list of baby names. It needed to be strong and stand out, but fit in. Toward the end of the list, I had written Louis. The first time I heard the name was from a character in a book my uncle used to read to my brother and me, The Ears of Louis. Embarrassed by the size of his ears, Louis learns to cope with school bullies while on a journey of self-discovery. He is strong-willed and stubborn, finding his way in the world when he doesn't quite fit in. My brother and I listened to the homemade book on tape during long car rides. I remember the driving more than the details of the story, but it's a memory that stuck with me.

I added Louis to the bottom of the list and forgot about it. As we filtered through each name, tossing out the ones that didn't feel right, we landed on Louis. We didn't know anyone else named Louis. It was easy to say and spell. Dan then added his own middle name—his grandmother's maiden name (which took some convincing on my part).

Louis DeWitt Ribbens. We let it linger for four days before writing it down on his birth certificate. The name felt strong because it was his own. With the ink drying on the official paperwork, I was discharged from the hospital. Louis was required to stay in the NICU for close monitoring.

We went home without our son. I felt a sinking relief to get home, immediately followed by guilt for leaving him. The ceremonial walk to the car felt empty and sad. As I carefully lowered my body into the car, I caught a glimpse of the empty car seat glaring back at me.

I quickly learned to manage the breast pump at home, filling out mother and baby information on the hospital labels for freezer storage bags. I would rinse out the equipment and set it all up to repeat the process every few hours. Each session became a distinct reminder that Louis was not there with us. At a time when I should have been bonding with my child, we were separated, both doing our best to improve his odds of survival.

I felt the need to prove my strength, foregoing the use of a wheelchair, opting to walk instead. We clocked hours in the hospital as if we worked there. I pumped on a firm schedule to earn my motherhood. All the while, Dan worked hard to find his space in between what Louis and I needed. He would change and wrap Louis up and hand him over to me, then sprint to the cafeteria for a hot lunch or dinner or midnight snack.

The nurses constantly encouraged us to get home for rest if we could. One evening we reluctantly agreed, with the promise of nursing Louis in the morning followed by his first bath. Up until then, Louis' fluid balance was meticulously monitored, not allowing me the ability to nurse him. Glued to my pump, I had hoped for a day when we might get the opportunity. Content to leave with something to look forward to, a normal first, we went home.

The next morning, we arrived at Louis' room to find the nurse burping him with an empty bottle of formula nearby. Tender and full in my chest, I knew he had been hungry. As a new mother, meeting his basic needs was the one thing I longed to provide. Louis was too full to feed and now I couldn't hold him because I needed to pump to relieve myself. Another taste of defeat in motherhood.

We moved on to give him his first bath. Dan carefully undressed and unplugged Louis, gently removing stickers and leads. Louis, a dusky shade of blue, reminded us how fragile he was. His smooth tiny frame filled Dan's hands. The nurse turned off his monitors and poured warm water into a clear rectangular bin with a miniature fitted sheet over the top. This allowed his body to stay submerged in the water, keeping his head afloat and his body warm. She pulled the sheet up at one corner to keep the water accessible. Dan gingerly lowered our naked baby onto the sheet and into the bin. The nurse wet his arms and legs, showing us how to lather the soap. She carefully but assertively took the soap from me to demonstrate proper hair washing, and in turn, stole another one of our firsts as a family of three.

Something delicate and new became a battle of wills between this over-confident nurse and me—a stubborn new mother. I wanted to stretch my new maternal muscles, yet everywhere I stepped, I was met with someone telling me what to do and how to do it. These seemingly inconsequential slights threatened my confidence. She challenged my competence. If I couldn't properly bathe my child, how would I muddle through what was coming next? With a deep breath, I swallowed my tears.

We carefully dried Louis, dressed him and wrapped him in a swaddle blanket. At least his blanket smelled like me, I thought. I pulled my hair back, shuffled over to one of the comfortable recliner chairs near his isolette and lowered myself to sit. As I let myself sink into the seat, I leaned back, expecting the chair to catch me. But it reclined farther than my body was able to stretch. It felt like someone forcefully sliced me in two with a red-hot spike. I doubled over as quickly as I could, cradling my belly. Dan looked at me with concern. Breathless, I whimpered, "too far." I couldn't feed him, bathe him, or sit properly in a chair. My physical pain finally matched my emotional anguish. Layers of defeat crashed over me, and the tears fell silently.

I couldn't care for myself or my child.

I sat folded in half for a while, until I felt ready to check my stitches. Little dots of bright red stained my bandages, a reminder that both Louis and I needed extra care. This day hurt and it had only just started. My emotional and physical tolerance had been pushed past their limits. I realized I had to slow down to allow Dan and the nurses to take care of both Louis and me.

Hoping the next day would turn things around, we arrived at the hospital in time to catch the doctors on their morning rounds, with a promise of going home! A larger discussion with our full care team felt it best to let Louis go home for a few weeks. He was doing well, not needing any medical interventions. The best next step would be to allow Louis to grow at home. To get stronger before his open-heart surgery. The idea scared me, but also brought some relief from the experience of the day before. The clouds had parted and a slice of sunlight shined through. Louis' next bath would be on my time. It meant his feeding schedule would be when he told me he was hungry, that instead of waking to pump and label and refrigerate, I could listen for my baby to cry out for me. Then I could step into his room… HIS room, lift him from his crib, and nurse him in the comfort of the rocking chair his grandpa refinished for him.

We would make our own schedule and get to know our baby, washing away the defeat of the day before. That was all I wanted. A diagnosis of congenital heart defects at thirty-two weeks gestation put all my motherhood plans on hold. I accepted that my baby would need heart surgery. Though completely foreign and terrifying, the science made sense. I understood. What I hadn't expected was how hard the in-between would be, the waiting and the variables I had no control over.

I thought having a baby wouldn't change much in my daily life. I would adjust for naps and feeding schedules, but things would otherwise remain the same. Before official hospital discharge could happen, we went over all potential signs of distress; change in skin color (dusky/blue), frequent vomiting/spit up, becoming more lethargic. All of that seemed like average baby behavior, reminding me that nothing about motherhood would be what I had expected. My first time at home with my own newborn—could I be trusted to discern normal baby behavior from cardiac distress?

Home

Louis had a full cardiac exam before leaving the hospital. We scheduled weekly visits with the cardiologist at the Pediatric Congenital Heart Center, as well as a check-in with our pediatrician. It was a lot of planning and paperwork, which felt bittersweet. This unexpected hurdle was conquered, but it was unclear how long the race was or how many obstacles remained.

We went home with strict instructions to monitor Louis for any signs of distress—feeding trouble, lethargy, labored breathing. They sent a car seat technician out to the parking garage with us. She made sure our car seat was installed properly and secured it in the backseat. She congratulated us, said goodbye and sent us on our way.

As we drove out of the hospital parking garage, I watched the first glimmer of sunlight grace Louis' cheeks. His first taste of sunshine and he greeted it with a scowl. Our inaugural ride home was short and uneventful and liberating. We drove straight home—a full two miles. I turned to check on Louis every fifteen seconds, grateful for the short, six-minute drive. He surveyed his surroundings, not focusing on anything in particular, safe between the straps of his car seat and tucked in with a gray, striped receiving blanket. He wore a navy blue hat that nearly covered his eyes. He hovered at seven pounds and seemed incredibly delicate, but we were going home.

Dan helped me out of the car then wrestled with the buckles to free Louis. He was eager to give our son a tour of our home. They walked around the yard first. They found their way inside through the kitchen where we warmed up a bottle of milk. I pulled some soup from the freezer and warmed it on the stove for dinner. Father and son continued their tour moving through the living room where we would spend our afternoons together. Dan carried him up the stairs to his bedroom, where he would sleep. I had surrendered any preconceived ideas of what my motherhood might look like while we waited for open-heart surgery. But now that we had permission to be home, I wanted a few things to go the way I imagined, starting with Louis sleeping in his crib. It had a gray jersey linen sheet, comfortably soft and sleep-safe. We filled his room with gifted stuffed animals, colorful board books and gender-neutral swaddle blankets. We had a fancy baby monitor with terrible reception. We kept the doors of our tiny Jack & Jill bathroom wide open, connecting our room to his. All three of us woke every few hours; I pumped after feeding Louis while Dan changed and swaddled him back to sleep. Sometimes, it was easy to forget Louis was sick. We had what appeared to be a perfect baby doing all the things babies do. It was hard to think about going back to the hospital for surgery, how it would feel for doctors to take my baby away again. Not thinking about what was next kept me going.

Our first weekly check-up came quickly. We drove to the heart clinic for a scheduled appointment. These visits included an exam of all vital signs, a blood pressure check with a cuff the size of a newborn sock, measurements of height and weight. The nurse buzzed around the room— moving machines on wheeled carts to and from Louis on the vinyl exam table. Still so little, unable to roll, he laid there, mesmerized by the brightness of the lights on the ceiling. Dan hovered over Louis, like a Lord guarding his treasure, ensuring its safety. The nurse worked methodically from one machine to the next. Placing a few stickers on his chest and another to his foot. This brand-new routine would become a familiar process, providing comfort and consistency in his care.

Louis was stable. His heart looked the same—still in need of surgery but functioning with appropriate blood flow. He was gaining weight. His blood oxygen saturations were within his usual range. Most people have an oxygen saturation between 95 and 100 percent. For Louis, with a heart condition that hinders the flow of oxygenated blood, his saturations were between 70 and 85 percent. We confirmed the details of our next appointment and headed back home. The first three weeks home were uneventful—each check-up identical to the last. Louis remained stable. All the time in between was spent learning about our son and stretching our parenting muscles. Things began to level out. We were managing a schedule that allowed all of us rest and recovery, showers and sustenance.

At our second weekly check-up with cardiology, we had a surgical consult with the lead pediatric heart surgeon, Dr. Haw. We sat in his tiny office, surrounded by models of anatomical hearts and anatomy books. He waltzed into the room, grazing the threshold of the doorway with his height, filling the room with confidence. Despite the need to hold a bisected heart model explaining procedures, his British accent made everything sound elegant and pleasing. He drew a diagram I couldn't decipher but we left his office feeling a little lighter, knowing someone could make Louis' heart stronger.

Dan had recently transitioned to work for himself as a web developer. He worked overtime during my third trimester, making it easy for him to take time off at home. Because we knew our baby would be born needing complex surgery, he had prepared to be away from the office for three months. With his work schedule on pause, we were able to focus strictly on our family. We used this time to learn how to parent. We flustered over the bewitching hour, taking turns consoling Louis' tired cries. We learned to change diapers quickly. Louis was growing, filling in his newborn clothes. The days ran together as we studied the features of his skin and memorized the weight of his body in our arms. We worked together, meeting our baby's needs, taking turns picking up the slack in house chores, and letting Louis nap on our chests.

One day, between check-ups, our cardiologist, Dr. Sowinski, called to check in. She noticed my area code was from the east side of the state and asked where I was from. I generally assume no one has heard of the small town where I went to high school, but I mentioned it anyway.

"I'm from Commerce too," she said. "Which high school did you go to?"

"Walled Lake Central," I replied.

"Me too! I bet my brother Eric was in your grade."

Though our paths had never crossed, it turned out that her brother and I had been in the same French class for three years. Common ground strengthened our caregiver-patient bond and it began to feel like friendship. We arrived at the next cardiac check-up with new confidence. Dan and I stood near Louis, reviewing the week we'd had at home.

The clinic nurse assured us that Dr. Sowinski would be in to review the results after one last test done with a handheld pulse oximeter. A small sensor is taped to a digit (finger or toe) and reads the oxygen saturation of the patient's blood. These meters are notorious for giving inaccurate readings from a wiggly foot, bad placement or a loose sticker. Attached to Louis' foot, the monitor flashed a pulse ox read of sixty-five (it's usually between ninety and one hundred for people without a heart condition). We weren't alarmed by this reading and insisted to the nurse that his numbers are usually in the eighties. She replaced the sticker and wrapped the sensor back around his toe. The screen lit up a bright red sixty-five for a second time. She excused herself and quickly returned with a rolling cart, the larger and more accurate pulse oximeter. She shut off her machine as quickly as it had arrived, wheeled it to the door and excused herself again.

Dr. Heather arrived a few minutes later. Petite and smartly dressed with black-framed glasses and straight shoulder-length brown hair, her empathy filled the room before she spoke. It was always reassuring to see her. She began every appointment the same way—had we noticed Louis showing any signs of distress, sleeping more frequently, vomiting after eating, any change in skin color—from pink to gray? We both shook our heads. No, we hadn't noticed anything like that. After a deep breath, she gently explained that though Louis looked well, his pulse oxygen saturation had dropped into the 60s, which was too low for him to be sent home. The Pediatric Intensive Care Unit was working quickly to prepare a room for us. She explained that instead of waiting for surgery at home, we would stay in the hospital until it was time.

We had been living in the in-between, time that was stolen from the reality that Louis was sick. I looked at Dan, wide-eyed in shock. The inevitable was now pending; Louis needed constant monitoring to determine when he would have open-heart surgery. I grabbed Louis' blanket, secured his swaddle, and scooped him up close to my chest, providing us both a level of comfort. I don't recall what more was said but I will always remember the sincerity and empathy in Dr. Heather's expression—simultaneously making me want to throw up and ask for a hug. I didn't want her empathy, but I needed it and felt grateful to be in her care. She left us in privacy to absorb this information. She returned to escort us to the PICU. Louis stayed swaddled and asleep in my arms with his head on my shoulder and the weight of his body on my chest as we walked, navigating the hallway labyrinth of the hospital, unaware of what lay ahead.

PART III

Baptism

I carried Louis in my arms against my chest and Dan followed behind with our diaper bag and car seat. When we stepped off the elevator into the PICU, it felt like we had arrived in another universe. A sense of urgency resonated everywhere—serious and heavy. Soft smiles from strangers greeted us. Each room looked identical. I made a conscious effort to keep my gaze from peering into anyone else's room, only glancing and studying the empty ones as we rolled by. Desperate for connection but unsure where to find it, we kept our heads down.

It took a while to get Louis comfortable. The furniture in the room had been rearranged to make space for the isolette, the same tall, clear hospital crib from the NICU, in the center of the room. One blue reclining rocking chair for me and a small chair with a collapsible desk for Dan. Herds of doctors and nurses rushed around, adjusting monitors and beeping machines. It left little space for feelings.

The chaos came quickly and ended abruptly as the waiting began. Phone calls and emails updated our family about Louis' care. We were invited to stay for something we would grow to seek comfort in—evening rounds.

Rounds occurred at every shift change. On-duty staff would then inform the incoming team about the details for every patient's care. There was a one-on-one update for the individual nurse in each room, and then the major staff overseeing the PICU huddled outside each room: intensivists, physicians assistants, fellows, nurses, cardiologists, respiratory therapists and surgeons. Our first experience with evening rounds was uneventful.

Louis' team introduced themselves and marveled at his sweetness. The twenty-four-hour plan included a restful night of quiet feedings and minimal monitoring with expert eyes on the situation. They shared a medical history recap and status update. Together, they created an hourly care plan. Though scary, it felt comforting and encouraging to have their guidance. They recommended that we sleep at home since Louis was stable. He would have a boring night of feeding and sleeping. It would be best for us to get a full night's rest to come back refreshed in the morning. We would have a meeting then that would include tests and scans to create a surgical plan.

I took an assessment of my body. I rolled my shoulders back and closed my eyes. I took a deep breath. Exhausted from a day full of abrupt changes, Dan and I stood on either side of Louis' and whispered to him:

"Sweet dreams, Baby. All you have to do is rest and we'll be back in a bit with more blankets and pajamas for you. We love you. Good night."

We tucked him in and promised to return early the next morning. I felt a strong pull to stay, maybe a mother's intuition. He slept sweetly wrapped in his blanket, much like he would at home. No bells or monitors expressed concern. During labor and delivery, I chronicled time by seconds. Once we were home, I marked milestones in weeks. More serious now, we moved in increments of hours—all the while waiting for Louis to get sicker. Knowing he was in capable hands, we went home for rest.

After I brushed my teeth, I called the PICU. His nurse answered like we were old friends and told me with confidence that everything was exactly as we had left it. With that, we fell asleep.

Two hours later, my phone startled me awake, instantly filling my body with dread. It was a local number I didn't recognize. It must be the hospital. I sat up at the edge of the bed. Our nurse, with the same gentle demeanor, calmly told me that, while feeding, Louis had aspirated. He was having trouble keeping his oxygen saturation up. They would need to intubate. It would be a bedside procedure to sedate him and insert a breathing tube attached to a ventilator that would push oxygen into his lungs. She explained a ventilator can allow a body to rest and regain strength. All standard in intensive care.

I felt like a teenager—the pink burning shame of confusion and fear flooding my face. Unsure of what to say, I uttered, "Okay." My panic weighed so heavy I couldn't think straight. My first lesson in self-preservation. To make it to the next minute, I couldn't acknowledge the fear pounding in my chest. I asked if we should come back. She assured us we did not need to. We weren't allowed in the room during a bedside procedure. She would call back within the hour when he was successfully on the ventilator. Another first followed—I questioned what to do next.

Dan sat wide awake beside me, trying to read my expression. Apprehensive in our feelings, we huddled side by side at the edge of the bed. We discussed returning to the hospital but decided to wait for the callback. Stunned, afraid to move, afraid to take a deep breath, we waited. Twenty minutes later, the phone rang again, sending terror through our veins. Dan pressed his head to mine and we listened together. Louis' intubation went well. Sedated to keep him still and comfortable, we were told we could stay home. No further changes were expected.

Louis would rest.

That was it.

The next step toward surgery.

And I wasn't there.

And I was in over my head.

Unable to quiet our uneasiness, we lay in bed, somewhere between asleep and awake. Wordless, we watched the sky grow lighter until the sun rose, giving permission to begin the day. We took the short drive to the hospital and again walked the labyrinth leading to the eighth floor. The elevator binged and the door slid open. We stepped into the lobby of the PICU, waved our badges as a set of double doors opened to a world of medical bustle. Blue scrubs and white coats marched by, faces armed with empathy and intention. We retraced our steps back to Louis' bedside. We slid the wide, glass door open and washed our hands at the sink. Using the foot pedal to turn on the water, I let it heat up as hot as my hands could stand it. One of the few things I could control, I scrubbed to wash away the fear I couldn't shake.

I took inventory of the room. Things looked more serious than they had just eight hours before. Machines I didn't recognize and foreign beeps I couldn't identify now existed. When we left, Louis had three stickers attached to his chest, casting a rhythmic pattern of green and red waves on the bedside monitor. Since we tucked him in, several more wires and monitors had arrived. First, a long flexible tube kept in place with a mustache of white tape across his upper lip, anchored at his cheeks. The tube ran from his mouth to a separate machine. It gently hummed a mechanical pattern of inhales and exhales. Another machine recorded each breath—blue numbers and shark fin graphs sliding across the screen.

Threaded through his nose, down into his belly, an orange feeding tube was taped to one side of his face. A flesh-colored sticker, wrapped around his big toe with a long white cord ran to the main screen overhead—the pulse oxygen monitor. His left arm extended perpendicular to his body, secured to a long flat board to keep him from bending. This was for the arterial IV line on his wrist to dispense medication that kept him asleep. And another line still, the PICC line—thin and clear stitched to the smooth pale skin of his left shoulder, with syringes full of clear fluids sending blood pressure medication directly to the veins of his heart.

Among these whirring machines and plastic tubes, I observed the frame of my tiny baby. Wearing only a diaper, the isolette's warming function kept him comfortable. With lines and cords in every direction, he couldn't wear the clothes I had brought for him.

Dan and I were eager for morning rounds to give us more information. We needed these machines to make sense. The team started at the opposite end of the PICU, twelve patients ahead of us. Unable to hold Louis in the meantime, the waiting hurt. The day before, I had been able to meet the needs of my son. The next morning, all I could do was lean on the advice of a dozen experts.

Finally, the medical team gathered around the entrance to Louis' room. His nurse slid the door open wide to include Dan and me. Intimidated but eager, we stepped closer, joining the semi-circle. The conversation began with the nurse, the same as yesterday, rattling off Louis' statistics, "Louis Ribbens, four weeks old, congenital heart disease, Transposition of the Great Arteries (TGA), Double Outlet Right Ventricle (DORV), Ventricular Septal Defect (VSD), Pulmonary Stenosis (PS), sating in the low sixties, admitted after routine cardiology check-up, was at Q4 feeds of breastmilk by bottle. Intubated overnight after aspiration. We are now holding breastmilk by NG and providing TPN through IV for fluid resuscitation..."

I stopped listening.

I heard everything she said but understood only half

of it. When the word, "resuscitate," landed in my ears, it felt like the air had been sucked out of my lungs. The room shrunk. I had trouble focusing my eyes on any one thing as they filled with tears. My ears rang. There wasn't enough oxygen in the room for me to take a deep breath.

Someone caught me before I fell to the ground. Someone else rushed to bring a chair. A woman in a purple shirt, a Child Life volunteer, ran over with juice and crackers. Too overwhelmed to protest, I accepted all of it. I was having a panic attack. The weight of what was coming, coupled with the escalation of the last twenty-four hours had me swallowed up in a dark worry.

Fluid resuscitation is very different from cardiac resuscitation. I would learn the difference and know the feelings of both. With Louis growing sicker each day, they added another machine—a nitric ventilator. The lead doctor, the intensivist, introduced himself as Dr. Boville, but insisted we call him Brian. With a reassuring face and booming voice, he commanded the room with intelligence, experience, and empathy. He must have seen the fear in my eyes after telling us our son was too sick for surgery.

"In the PICU, we bring out every avenue of support at once," he said. "And then slowly take each one away as we see improvement. I know this looks scary. I want you to know that I have more avenues to explore for Louis. I am not worried. I will tell you when I am worried."

He fixed his kind blue eyes on my face and counseled me, "Right now, I need you to know that I am not worried."

He said it all so matter-of-factly with ease and confidence. I had no choice but to believe him.

This memory still comforts me.

Without regular movement, Louis retained IV fluid. He lay motionless, bloated, nearly unrecognizable. I did my best to care for him, managing diaper changes and holding him with my index finger in the palm of his hand. I wanted to pray but I didn't know where to start.

Catholics believe in sacraments, ceremonial prayers of religious rites. Because God is present in the sacraments and through them, there can be physical and spiritual healing. Sacraments are performed to provide grace and care through faith—invisible realities. There are special prayers and oils and gestures, celebrations and reconciliations. One of these ceremonies is baptism, symbolic of purification, a rite of regeneration through the water. Without baptism, it is thought that a soul can't enter the kingdom of God. I never said it out loud because I wasn't sure I believed it. But, if Louis wasn't going to survive and his soul would be stuck in purgatory, never at rest, I wasn't willing to risk it. I called Father G from the Catholic Cathedral downtown, and left a rather panicked introduction and pleading voicemail.

The PICU receptionist called Louis' room to tell us we had a visitor. I straightened my sweatshirt and smoothed my hair back before heading to the front desk to greet him. Sliding the heavy glass door open, I met Father G in the hallway and introduced myself. We shook hands. He wore plain clothes and somehow looked smaller than I had remembered. At Sunday mass, in a giant ornate cathedral draped with holy cloaks, he looked colossal. Wandering down the PICU labyrinth, mildly overwhelmed, bewildered by fluorescent lights and the constant and urgent beeping against the somber tone of the entire floor—he looked like an old man.

I wanted to prepare Father G for what he was about to see, the seriousness of Louis' medical condition. I stuttered, stumbling over what to say and how to say it. I started with the details of Louis' heart condition and that we had to wait for Louis to get stronger before the surgeon, Dr. Haw, could perform open-heart surgery. As we approached Louis' room, I slid the heavy glass door open and invited him in. Dan, my parents, Louis' godmother Ashley (a close friend of mine), and a nurse, all greeted him. We showed Father G how to use the foot pedal-controlled sink to wash his hands. As he walked further into the room, he got a closer look at Louis.

"Judas priest!" he called out.

I surprised myself with an unexpected laugh. There was something about what he said and how he said it (or who he was) that surprised me. Judas priest, it WAS a lot to take in. Louis was just a few weeks old and so sick. So sick. Looking at my darling baby, other people first saw how fragile he was, how close to dying he seemed. And though I knew how serious his condition was, I wouldn't allow my mind to consider any alternative to surviving.

Judas priest.

Father G began in prayer by reciting the baptismal rights. We gathered around Louis to reject Satan, all his empty works and promises. Father G anointed Louis' forehead with consecrated oil while reciting, "Bless this oil and sanctify it for our use. Make this oil a remedy for all who are anointed with it; heal them in body, in soul, and in spirit, and deliver them from every affliction."

He concluded with a blessing and anointing of the sick—another sacrament. A ministry of comfort, anointing usually occurs when a person is in danger of death, from illness, or old age. The entire experience took no more than fifteen minutes.

The ritual of surrender to prayer and the ceremony of baptism filled me with comfort and rage. I felt comfort in preparing Louis' body for battle and his spirit for rest, while also cursing a God who would allow my son to suffer—sick before he was even born.

Please God, heal him.
Body and soul and spirit.
Deliver him back to my arms.
In this life, let me learn who he is.
In this life, let me be his mother.

I didn't want to believe in a god that handed out illnesses like parking tickets. It mattered less what I believed and more what I could do to promote wellness. Despite my doubt, I welcomed this sacrament of healing and reconciliation in the hopes of holding my son again.

There was no baptismal celebration—no party with gifts and cake. There were no family photos in christening gowns. We spent this day in an idle Hail Mary. Louis' baptism was an effort to safeguard him against death or to ensure his path to heaven. We ended the day in relief with renewed hope for another day, one step closer to open-heart surgery, trying to forget that nothing guaranteed survival.

We all thanked Father G, then Dan and I escorted him back through the hall to the lobby. Dan and I mentioned our intentions to be married and how we had other (obviously) pressing things demanding our attention. He gave me his phone number and email and told me not to wait to call him, making himself available in support of our son and our family. The rest of the evening passed quietly.

The moment of cleansing and baptism had given me permission to acknowledge the feelings of fear and grief that had been consuming me. Sad and mad and desperate, I found comfort in Father G's presence. I taped a tiny prayer relic of Father Solanus inside Louis' isolette. I can't remember exactly what Father G said. I wasn't ready to pray for the soul of my son. I focused on my breathing, on holding back tears. I knew I needed Father G to be there for Louis, not for me. I could cry later. I had ritually prepared my baby's soul for whatever would come next. Facing that impossible yet possible reality had been unbearable.

Open-Heart Surgery

For nine days, we spent all our waking hours in the PICU. We began calling his room Louis' Office. Our routine was always the same—we'd set our things down, wash our hands and greet Louis. I'd slowly step further into his room, wedged between the nurse's computer and his isolette. I opened the closet to hang my backpack—my breakfast of coffee and yogurt already forgotten at the sink.

When the evening nurse updated the daytime nurse on his care, they spoke in a quiet whisper. I overheard terms like "bouts of SVT." I looked around the room to distract myself from listening. Someone had changed his pillowcase. This one was soft and green with animated rabbits smiling at us. If it weren't for all the monitors and tubes and cords and incessant beeping, you might think he was simply sleeping. But you couldn't ignore the machines doing the work of his body while the medications kept him asleep.

With his planned surgery scheduled for the next day, Louis' care team decided it would be best to push the surgery again. He wasn't strong enough yet. While we thought the day would include a preoperative bath with preparations for surgery, instead it became another day of waiting. We waited for him to get sicker and now he was too weak for surgery. He needed more time. We'd try again next week.

Another week of waiting meant we still couldn't hold him. I felt my cheeks burn and my eyes well with tears. A commotion sparked outside of our room. Grateful for a distraction, I watched a nurse set her small patient onto a mat in the hallway. Surrounded by toys, this little girl looked about six months old and she had never left the hospital. Later in the day, I read from a mom support blog about someone's lousy day of carpooling and traffic and napless babies. I longed to feel what I imagined was the sweet sleep deprivation that comes with a healthy newborn at home. Our eternity had only been two weeks. We existed somewhere between two extremes—not living and not dying, but in a purgatory of dormant dread. Stuck in a holding pattern, we pushed our defeat aside and resigned ourselves to wait.

A Child Life Specialist surprised us with a banner he'd hung on the wall near the glass door. In large blue letters surrounded with polka dots, it read, "Louis' Office." The tears I'd been saving overwhelmed me like a thunderstorm, unexpected and all at once. It was such a thoughtful and lighthearted gesture. And it filled me with apprehension. I didn't want to be comfortable here.

Still, I savored the moment.

When we first learned about Louis' heart condition, zpeople encouraged me to find support groups online. I searched a few and joined the ones that seemed relevant: Heart Moms, Transposition of the Great Arteries, Michigan Pediatric CHD. Filled with seasoned parents who've navigated decades of surgeries and medical interventions, their posts exceeded my experience. I skimmed through pages of posts and comments asking for advice. Failed surgical interventions, strokes, life-long limitations, comfort care, feeding tubes—all of it frightened me. I immediately hid it all from my Facebook newsfeed. I was too fragile to try to work through anyone else's experience, especially when mine came mixed with fear and heartbreak.

A few posts trickled through and I offered advice on breastfeeding through a hospital admission. I saw a few posts celebrating heartiversaries—anniversaries of heart surgeries past. And then the internet reminded me that it has no filter.

A woman posted in utter distress. She and her husband were expecting their first child. They were hoping to find out their baby's gender at their twenty-week ultrasound to complete their nursery in blue or pink. Instead, she was given an unexpected CHD diagnosis. Her baby needed heart surgery.

Her fear was real.

Sitting beside my son on life support, I understood her angst as I read her words.

"I did everything right," she said. "We did everything right. We dated for several years. We had a long engagement. We abstained until our wedding night. We did everything we were supposed to. We don't deserve this. Why is this happening to me? Our baby is supposed to be healthy. Why would God do this to me?"

She had unknowingly taken a stab at a tender wound of mine. A wound still healing. That either of us, or our children, were deserving of such suffering felt cruel. And that was not the kind of mercy I believed in. She used shame and God to justify bad things happening to other people—people like me. This stranger's judgment swallowed me up. If we both believed in the same god, then he was misleading one of us.

I stopped checking the support groups for advice.

A week later, on the morning of the rescheduled surgery, Dan and I woke earlier than usual and quietly moved through the motions of our simplified morning routine. We skipped breakfast and methodically threw our socks and shoes on. Equipped with our parent badges and parking passes, we drove to the hospital in silence. The short drive felt like a lifetime. We took our usual route from the parking structure to the elevator to the bridge. Watching the traffic below, I wondered if any of those travelers' days were as monumental as ours. There's always the chance of an emergency pushing planned surgeries back. No news meant things moved as planned. All possibilities of the day hung heavy in the air.

We arrived before shift change and were granted a small gift. We were able to hold Louis. It took two nurses to organize the cords and monitors. We each got a turn to hold him, albeit unable to rock or pat or make any sudden movements. Dan shortened his turn to give me a second one. While I held Louis for a second time that morning, the room filled with doctors and nurses in blue surgical scrubs.

Gazing down at my son, his body half the length of the pillow beneath him, I wanted time to stand still. I tried to memorize the way he felt, the way he smelled. But nothing was his own. Swallowed with cords, flanked by machines, covered in surgical tape—I couldn't memorize him, I couldn't know him until we could take him home from here, after this surgery.

Medical staff filed in one by one, serious and somber and kind. The lead surgeon, Dr. Haw, entered first, followed by two operating room nurses, an anesthesiologist, and three ICU nurses, all ready to deliver pre- and post-op instructions.

Dr. Haw, sincere and thorough, went over Louis' complicated procedure for a third and final time with us, complete with hand-drawn diagrams. He told us that in his career he had performed this operation three hundred times. He went on to say that he'd performed between ten and twenty with complexities like Louis' heart, and he had lost three of those patients.

Dan had the presence of mind to ask a few details about those losses and we learned those patients had other complications. It didn't feel like relief, but it was something. Up until that moment, I hadn't considered an actual mortality statistic based on the surgeon's experience and outcomes. I felt sick. I wanted to run screaming out of the room with Louis in my arms. I wouldn't stop until he and I were safe somewhere, together forever. But I couldn't move. I focused my gaze on Louis. Uncontrollably, tears streamed down my face. I knew the safest place for him was not in my arms. The safest place for him was in the hands of this surgical team, who would do their best to improve his health and give us years to grow together.

There were no other options. This was it. This was happening and my job was to surrender. We signed several pages of paperwork I didn't bother reading. I know they explained each waiver and the procedure in detail, but I don't remember what they said. I was busy turning over the survival statistics in my head and kicking myself for not asking about those specifics sooner. Questions flooded my mind, second-guessing my own judgment.

Had we done the work of diligent parents?

Was the surgery going to succeed?

Would our child survive the day?

I spoke to him in a hushed tone, cradled in my arms. "You've had time to rest, Louis. Now it's time to fight. The medicine and these doctors are working to make your body stronger, but you need to push."

I needed him to persevere.

"I'll be right here waiting for you to come back. I need you to come back. I love you." And then, placing my trust in a team of people we'd only just met, Dan and I whispered life over Louis and handed him over.

Waiting

The surgeons and nurses wheeled his isolette down the hall and silence saturated Louis' Office. The absence of noisy machines became a glaring reminder of all that I couldn't control. I held agony in my heart. An unsettling combination of terror and sadness and unconditional love. Fear grew heavier than hope, delicate like a playground teeter-totter. The next few hours would determine the fate of our young family.

Dan and I took a slow walk to the basement—the home of the surgical waiting room, the emergency department and the radiology lab. We stopped at the reception desk where the attendant gave us a postcard-sized piece of paper with a number written on it. Alongside the number was a colorful graph listing the steps of surgery. Further into the waiting room, there were monitors displaying these numbers in a corresponding color, allowing us to track our child's progress while maintaining anonymity. Dan and I agreed this step would only make us more anxious, so I tucked the paper away, never reading the number assigned to our son.

We already knew that hospital time doesn't pass like hours on a clock or calendar. Hospital time moved at the speed of medicine and sickness. Surgery would take many hours, the first three used to prepare the room and body for the procedure. Hours would pass before we would hear any news, with more waiting between each update.

We spent the better half of the day in the waiting room, gazing out along a sloping five-lane boulevard. Dissecting the city, traffic congested the road all waking hours. City buses, ambulances, semi-trucks, and SUVs all whizzed by, unaware of the families in agony beside them. I'd driven by these windows a thousand times, always admiring the architecture, never noticing the faces on the other side of the glass. Along the road, the windows of the hospital float like slow waves cascading the length of the building. The design created a beau-tiful organic shape in a city made of concrete. It wasn't until I stood on the inside looking out that I realized what the room on the main floor was for—the space in-between, full of anguish and hope.

I tried to keep my mind empty, away from the what-ifs. A hollow head can quickly become a dark place. I focused on the mundane—cars passing by. I counted them. I cataloged the make and model and colors of each vehicle. My former self would have surrendered to prayer, but I refused. I couldn't concede that God had a plan if it didn't include Louis' survival and there were no guarantees. Talking to God felt like a plea for a sinner's absolution. Louis was not a sinner. He was a baby. He was made new. I needed the surgeons to make Louis' heart whole, not God. Prayer felt like begging.

Dan stayed busy writing emails to friends and family

with updates on Louis. I had brought a thick pack of origami paper, vibrant in color. There's an ancient Japanese legend promising a wish or miracle granted by the gods to anyone who folds a thousand paper cranes—a symbol of peace. I was willing to pray to anyone's God but mine, so I started folding. Creating each crane brought its own peace, soothing and simple. It had immediate results. With no way to encourage a favorable outcome, I felt desperate. I kept folding.

After I completed each crane, I dropped it into a clear plastic Ziploc bag beside my feet. The act became meditative. I folded deep purples and radiant reds. I bent through bold greens and glowing yellows, pleating each wing between my thumbs. With every crease I pushed away any thoughts that didn't center on living.

We watched other families enter the waiting room and subsequently be escorted out. About an hour in, a nurse came to update us on Dr. Haw's progress. I surveyed her as she walked over to us. The room felt like the length of a dozen football fields, giving me time to analyze every inch of her face. Her walk, confident. Her face, smiling. She didn't waste time with any polite greetings.

"He's doing well," she said.

Thank God, or gods, or science, or luck.

My ears began to buzz the way fluorescent lights do, reminding me to breathe deeply. Over the next several hours the same nurse repeated the same walk and the same words in the same way, "steady as he goes." Hoping no news meant good news, yet desperate for an update, we were frozen in our waiting.

On her final visit, she escorted us to the post-op consultation room. With a reassuring smile, she left us to wait for Dr. Haw. Barely the length of my car, the room felt tiny. A forgettable shade of beige covered the walls. A large monitor mounted to the wall faced a set of chairs. Tucked in next to them was a side table with a lamp and a box of tissues. We sat down in the chairs as the door clicked shut behind us. I noticed another door, opposite the entrance. I heard footsteps passing beyond that door and wondered where they were headed. I wondered how many families had received bad news here. I wondered if we would join that statistic.

Dr. Haw entered, looking confident and focused. I scanned every detail of his expression, his posture, the air he brought into the room, searching for any indication of what he might say next. He began by explaining the procedure, as he had done several times before.

"Louis is doing fine," he said. "Everything went well."

This man had held our son's heart in his hands and the surgery was over. Things were different this time because we weren't speaking of eventualities or hypothetical outcomes. This part of it was now in the past—something that had already happened. We were addressing our reality.

Dr. Haw described the most complex part of the surgery, relocating Louis' coronary arteries. He compared the size of an infant's heart to a strawberry. I looked down at my own hand and imagined I could hold three or four strawberries in each palm. He went on to say each coronary artery is about a millimeter in size, like the tip of a freshly sharpened pencil. He cut around the vessel carefully, with enough tissue to stitch them in a new location.

I think of a surgeon as someone confident, an experienced scientist in a lab, measuring outcomes and recording data, analyzing technique. But hearing him detail this delicate work, of moving vessels in infant hearts, revealed him to be more of an artist. He's a creator, studying each unique canvas and preparing his tools to tailor the passages of every heart. He's a mathematician, carefully calculating measurements of millimeters for proper blood flow. He's a plumber, creating and adapting the pipes and ducts to ensure life. I hadn't considered the scale of his skill—nuanced and necessary.

Dr. Haw reassured us that the surgery had gone as planned, so far. He reiterated that recovery is a process all its own. The next two days would prove critical for Louis' healing. While he shared the delicate nature of recovery and listed the things we would be closely monitoring, the surgical team settled Louis back into his office on the 8th floor in the intensive care unit. Thoughts of complications bounced around my head—critical coronary placement, recovering electrical function. The momentary relief turned to worry, and we prepared for more waiting.

This part of Louis' recovery feels foggy in my memory. Days blended. A full week passed without notice. Tiny improvements each day led to monumental changes—breathing tube removal, the start of bottle feeds, daily skin-to-skin sessions. We were taking turns holding him for hours at a time. I became familiar with the hospital breast pump and the freezer storage. One night we stayed into the late hours, not ready to say good night. I had stepped to the bathroom in our room to wash the parts of my breast pump in preparation for the next day. As I dried my hands, I heard a woman's gasping scream. The agony in her voice echoed through the wall. I stepped back into the main room, still able to hear the woman's muffled cries. A respiratory therapist had walked in while I was in the bathroom. Reading the concern on my face, she reluctantly shared that the child in the neighboring room had died. I froze for a moment. Without saying anything, I retreated back into the bathroom and placed my hand on the wall to the neighboring room. Though we had never met, I felt deeply for her loss. No words could communicate that, especially in her darkest hour, while my son lay nearby, alive and recovering.

I stood there a moment more and then went to Louis' side. He was warm and swaddled and resting. I had a chance to watch my child grow. I wouldn't waste my time wallowing in things we had lost, when so much had been restored.

Over the next few days, we monitored Louis closely, adjusting medications to account for the withdrawal he was exhibiting from the heavy narcotics, and performing scans and exams to ensure the surgery had been successful in restoring proper blood flow—all necessary steps to get us back home. Dan and I felt helpless. There was little we could do for Louis. As his medications lowered, he became more alert and we began singing and reading to him.

Dan and I took turns reading chapters from children's books, starting with *Charlie and the Chocolate*

Factory. Dan passed the novel to me, reminding me of which chapter we last read. I'd surrender my post in the oversized rocking chair to find a spot to stand. Poised between cords and monitors and Louis' isolette, I read quietly at first, nervous for nurses and passersby to overhear. I didn't recognize my own voice, unpracticed and timid, echoing around the sterile room. I kept reading. My insecurities melted as the story filled the room with candy visions and magic.

***

The following day, we were granted permission to take Louis home. Ten days after open-heart surgery, we left the hospital with Louis for the second time. Slower this time, with sternal precautions, timed medications, and palpable fear. Except for the fresh sterile bandage covering his battle wounds—a thin pink line of new flesh bound back together adorned with tight black stitches lining the length of his chest, Louis' body was the same on the outside. He had been made new on the inside, invisible stitches correcting the plumbing of his heart. I felt grateful to be through the worst of it and hoped like hell his body was rehabilitated. We would start again, teaching him to drink from a bottle, sleep in his crib, and take medication from a syringe on a schedule.

Several days later at home, we settled into our new anxieties in the careful keeping of our son. With Halloween quickly approaching, Dan and I recycled our costumes from the year before—a circus ringleader for Dan in a red blazer with gold stripes, a lion broach and top hat. He even shaved his beard into a mustache. I wore all beige and jumped into my homemade cardboard giraffe costume. We painted a mustache that curled up on the ends on Louis' top lip. He wore a striped singlet over his onesie, and I made a barbell out of a straw and round Styrofoam balls—our Strong Man. We handed out candy together on the front porch. Our joy emanated all around us. How lucky we were. At home, healthy and sharing in a normal first experience with our baby.

PART IV

Help

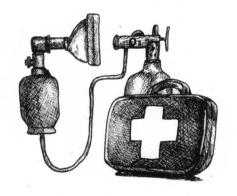

Another week at home meant establishing a routine. Dan would get up early and take Louis downstairs. He started a load of laundry and prepared breakfast, with milk and medicine for Louis. I savored the sleep-in, taking a few minutes to get dressed before joining them. From our bedroom window I could see the sun shining through gray November clouds.

Together in our bright yellow living room, Dan gave me the morning's inventory of things to know—feeding times and diaper changes.

"Louis had a big spit-up," Dan said. "I fed him, so I think it's just normal baby stuff." Dan handed Louis to me and I carefully cradled my baby in my arms. He dry heaved a little, so I sat him up. He threw up again. We cleaned him up in the kitchen sink the way they taught us in the NICU. We put clean clothes on Louis while discussing which doctor to call. Pediatrician? PICU intensivist? Cardiologist? Vomiting and lethargy can be signs of cardiac distress. Sleeping and spitting up are also what babies do.

Dan had stepped into the kitchen to sort through our hospital discharge paperwork, to find a phone number to call. Nervous but unable to decipher new parent nerves from instinct, I tried not to panic as I held Louis. I watched him close his eyes as every ounce of pink rushed out of his tiny body. Each inch of skin went gray. His breathing became shallow. His eyes gently closed and he went limp.

"CALL 911!" I screamed.

I held my infant son as he turned blue.

Dan's phone volume was loud. The dispatcher seemed too calm. She asked him questions that took too long and felt irrelevant. She repeated her questions for clarification while I watched the life drain from my son's body. I looked at Dan with urgency and dismay, desperate for the sound of sirens.

"Can you just get here?" He unlocked the front door.

I held Louis tightly. I stroked his feathery hair and whispered, "It's okay, Baby. You're alright, Louis. Stay with me."

A comfort for my own desperation.

Dan stayed on the phone for three long minutes before we heard sirens rapidly approaching. We confirmed the sirens with the 911 dispatcher and hung up. The high-pitched wailing sound, sharper and louder than before, headed for and stopped in front of our house. Alarming and urgent, the fire truck was the first to arrive with the ambulance close behind. As first responders came inside, Dan handed them the hospital discharge paperwork. We explained Louis' complex congenital heart condition and that he recently had open-heart surgery. As I gently handed him over, an EMT put an oxygen mask over Louis' pale face. They carefully placed him into his car seat. I ran blindly to the opposite end of the house for my socks and shoes, meeting them at the front door. I climbed into the ambulance as they loaded Louis onto the gurney in his car seat. I realized I hadn't seen Dan. They told me he would meet us in the emergency room and a streak of silver backed out of our driveway. He was already in the car and on his way.

I sat behind the ambulance driver, back-to-back, facing the open tailgate. Louis sat on the gurney in front of me. The angle of the stretcher, with Louis in his car seat, obstructed any sight of him. I watched every move the EMTs and firefighters made as they fumbled to find infant-sized equipment. They were calm, assuring me that Louis' color had returned after placing the oversized oxygen mask on his face.

Feeling the cold metal under my feet, I remembered my bare feet. I grabbed the socks shoved into my pocket and haphazardly slipped them on my feet, jammed on my boots, and began tying my laces as the ambulance door slammed shut. From the corner of my eye, I felt splashes of sunlight. Glancing out of the tiny window, I heard blaring sirens echoing above my head.

The route to the Children's Emergency Department takes six minutes. We pulled into a garage where Dan was waiting, wide-eyed in panic. When I climbed out of the ambulance he whispered, "What took so long?"

I assured him nothing more had happened. Louis was still very much alive, as far as I knew.

We followed Louis' stretcher into an exam room. A dozen people came flying in, calling out instructions, demanding equipment. Dan and I huddled together between two supply cabinets watching in helpless agony. Nurses, gentle but firm, stripped Louis of his clothes and discussed access for an IV. Each passing minute without more information felt eternal. Someone suggested we wait outside the room.

Ushered into the hallway, we stood in disbelief. A familiar face, our cardiac nurse, Amy, peered around the corner. With concern in her eyes, she hugged us both, "What's going on?" she asked.

"He threw up," Dan said. "And then went gray. We called 911 and now we're here."

"How did you know we were here?" I asked.

"When there is an incoming trauma call, it's shared with the PICU. Based on history and symptoms, I had a feeling it was Louis."

It felt good to have people know our track record, but painful to have such a history.

I can't say how long we waited for information. They checked all of Louis' vitals while preparing a room for him in the PICU. He was sedated and intubated and put on medications to manage his blood pressure. They would wheel him up to the PICU and prepare a room for us to stay a few days. A nurse instructed us to wait in the PICU lobby. We let the care team work, confident in their ability yet eager for more information.

Dan and I walked slowly through the familiar maze of hallways from the emergency room to the hospital's main lobby. Back at the security desk, we turned on our hospital autopilot to acquire parent badges and parking passes. We took that dreaded walk to the elevators, where a cheerful and familiar ding sent me deeper into despair. We stepped onto the elevator. As the door closed, the air flooded with the memory of childbirth, fears about the wellness of my baby. It hung there in the elevator with the smell of Purell. We arrived in the familiar lobby of the eighth floor, the Pediatric ICU. We gave our name to the receptionist. She kindly assured us someone would come to get us when Louis' room was ready.

One other family huddled in the corner of the lobby, speaking with their care team about the results of a recent procedure. Our nurse came over, introduced herself and walked us back to Louis' room. The same room he had been in just a few weeks before. We learned that Louis' heart rate was normal, but his heart rhythm was too fast. He had developed an arrhythmia called Supraventricular Tachycardia (SVT) which is an abnormally fast heart rhythm arising from improper electrical activity—atrial fibrillation, in the upper part of the heart.

I asked the PICU intensivist to explain his condition several times. The upper chambers of the heart were contracting so quickly that they were not filling the lower chambers properly, which caused Louis to become very pale. Heart rate is the number of times the heart beats in a minute. The heart rhythm is the pattern of the heartbeat. Normal rhythm is called sinus rhythm. They sedated Louis and began working on adjusting blood pressure medications to improve his heart function and rhythm. We would stay in the PICU for a series of tests over several days before we would have a medical plan.

After a few days of tests without any conclusive answers, I remembered that I needed to go and vote. Our

2016 presidential election—a big one. Louis was critical but stable, and I needed a reason to step out of the hospital for an hour. Standing in line at the local elementary school to cast my vote, a woman stood in front of me, cradling her baby in her arms—shushing her to sleep. Behind me, a woman held the hand of her oldest while pushing her toddler in a stroller. I was acutely reminded that I was missing something. Strangers smiled as they walked by. Each look became a glaring reminder that I stood alone in line. My baby, not at my side nor at home, but in the hospital. Sick.

The rest of that day, and the subsequent week, play in slow motion in my memory. Every second a snapshot, each image filled with greater fear than the one before.

ECMO

After a few critical but stable days, and dozens of tests with no answers, our care team decided to take Louis to the Catheterization Lab for a physical look at his heart. They would put a tiny camera through a femoral vein and explore the inside of his heart. This would be a more invasive look than imaging, like x-rays and CT scans, but less risky than open-heart surgery.

Dan and I found ourselves victims in the OR waiting room again. The soft-voiced receptionist gave us our postcard and gestured toward open seating. I scanned the waiting room wondering if the other parents could feel my anxiety or if I could sense theirs. We quietly whispered ways to occupy our time. He ran to the cafeteria for breakfast. It was later in the day than I had expected. Breakfast ended hours ago.

He returned with a plate full of snacks—hummus and carrot sticks, pita bread with cheese. I couldn't eat. I picked at some bread, but my feelings were all too familiar. I sat unmoving and listless with a belly full of dread. Without any clear answers, my mind was left to wonder and imagine the worst.

I needed to occupy my mind. I put the snack plate on

the coffee table in front of me and reached for the post-card shoved deep in the diaper bag. I memorized Louis' nine-digit number and looked for it on the monitor display. A little purple box read, "IN SURGERY." I was surprised. Usually, it would read "PREP" and then a nurse would come out to tell us when surgery began. I snapped a photo of the screen and walked back to my seat, wondering what it meant. Only forty-five minutes had passed since they took Louis to the cath lab—not enough time for surgery prep. I combed through all possible explanations while I watched a scrub nurse walk toward us. I considered all the ways a hospital might catalog a patient's surgical status. Who clicks the computer to change their status? A receptionist? A surgical intern in the OR? Whose computer do they use?

Her wide, sky-blue pant legs never creased as she glided towards us. Jolted from my thoughts by her gentle greeting, she explained that the heart cath showed Louis' coronary artery stretched too thin, limiting the blood flow to his heart, which could cause a heart attack. The surgeon needed to perform a repair and it needed to happen right away. They would know more once they had his chest open.

Louis was sicker than we thought. Shifting from fact-finding to lifesaving—there wasn't time to feel anything but panic.

The nurse's tone was kind yet compelling. Louis was intubated and sedated from the catheterization, so they would be moving him to the operating room now. The surgeon gave permission for us to see him while he was still in the cath lab, but we needed to move quickly.

The nurse led us down one fluorescently lit hallway to the next, until we stopped abruptly at a set of beige doors. They were indistinguishable from the rest of the double doors lining the hallway except for the sign in big red letters, "STERILE ROOM." Inside the room, large glowing white machines formidably flanked the walls on every side. In the center of the room stretched a long gray table and there on top, lying motionless, was our son. He looked so frail, plugged in and hooked up to several cords and tubes, all strung to monitors and medications hugging the length of the table. Dreams of my newborn existed in soft light and cozy spaces, warm blankets with comfortable furniture. This room? The opposite of those dreams. Cold and unforgiving. Everything you wouldn't want for a baby.

I didn't know where to stand or how to lean close to him.

I put my hand on his forehead, the only part of him free of machines and cords. I frantically scanned the room for something familiar, forcing my mind to express encouragement, despite the terror I felt. What would I say if this was the last time I would touch him? How do I tell him to keep living?

"I love you, Baby Bird. Mama's here, Baby Louis. You can do this."

I whispered to him as I gently ran my finger along his cheek. I didn't reach down to kiss him for fear of bumping unknown cords, surely supporting my child's life. I stepped aside to allow Dan his brief turn. We were back through the hallway and into the waiting room minutes later. Dan and I sat in silence, unsure of what we had just witnessed.

Questions that pain me still. Did they bring us back to say goodbye? Would that be the last I saw of my child, alive? Why didn't I bend down to kiss him?

I pushed these thoughts from my mind and turned my attention to things I could control. We went back to Louis' empty room in the PICU. Our photos lined the walls—cards from our family stacked in a pile on the counter, our pillows and books on the table near the recliner, an enormous gaping hole in the center of the room where his hospital bed and life support machines lived. It was dark and quiet. All screens and monitors were turned off. The normally incessant alarms were silent. A nurse sat at the desk catching up on paperwork, awaiting her tiny patient's return. The room felt void of life.

I surveyed the photos on the wall—Dan, Louis, and I in our Halloween costumes from just a few days ago, our first hike through the city park, our self-portrait taken the day Louis turned blue and first responders knocked at our door. I tore the photo of wide-eyed infant Louis from the wall and collapsed to the floor on my knees.

"Is this all we get?" I desperately called out to Dan.

Silently, I asked God the same thing, and then begged for it not to be. Without a word, Dan held me, both of us sobbing.

My child, my Pieta, except I was not willing to sacrifice him.

Several hours passed and we heard nothing. There were no updates from nurses. Back in the OR waiting room, we watched families come and leave again. I wondered what ailed their children—a broken arm, tonsil removal, stitches of the flesh. It wasn't until late into the night the nurse came and took us into the post-operative waiting room. I'll never forget the concern and defeat on Dr. Haws' face when he sat down to brief us of the results from the unexpected but necessary open-heart surgery.

Deep purple lines marked his hairline where the surgical cap had gripped his skin all these hours. His forehead was wrinkled with dismay, his brow furrowed, unable to find the why. His posture filled the chair and the room with experience and concern. He crossed his legs. I noticed the cuff of his left scrub pant leg was stained a dark rust color. I wondered if it was blood. I began listing potential products that would stain in such a way, praying it was betadine. I analyzed every word, each expression, any moment of hesitation.

Dr. Haw explained that he had intended to resect Louis' left coronary artery and shift the position to improve blood flow. Once inside Louis' chest he found the position of the artery was appropriate, but small adhesions of tissue were pushing on that tiny artery, restricting blood flow. He said the task of opening the chest to expose the heart usually takes an hour. In this instance, it took him three hours to reach Louis' heart because of these fibrous adhesions. The surgery was more involved and harder on the body than expected. He put Louis on a bypass machine called ECMO, to allow Louis' body to rest.

Dr. Haw explained that ECMO (extracorporeal membrane oxygenation) is a body machine. All it needs is blood. It helps the human body rest from physical trauma by performing the work of the heart and lungs. Louis needed ECMO because his body was tired. He had sustained some controlled stress but also some unforeseen complications to his heart. His infant body didn't have much strength reserved, especially since he was already recovering from open-heart surgery.

Louis' prognosis would be day by day. He would come off the machine when things improved, maybe in a few days—no more than two weeks. The surgical team was moving Louis back to intensive care, but because of the added machines, it would be a few hours before we could join him. Dr. Haw warned that the addition of the ECMO machine would crowd the room and create a need for an extra nurse.

Patients need a care team bigger than themselves—to bridge the gap in care they can't get at home. Caregivers need strength in numbers to encourage faith and hope and all the good feelings people require when in a crisis. When surrounded by darkness, in need of a sliver of light, we need our doctors to be giants.

The PICU keeps one nurse with the same patient each week, when they can, to establish consistent care. We got to know our nurse, Jon. He preferred the night shift, thriving as a night owl, working midnights for twenty years. He had a few daughters nearly through high school. He loved the movie, "O Brother Where Art Thou?" He had experience. Louis was not the first child he has seen knocking on death's door.

Jon's conversation became something I looked forward to, providing a sense of normalcy in a situation far from ordinary. I changed Louis' diaper, making conversation about upcoming holiday plans while Jon held the chest tubes so as not to disturb them—minor exchanges providing hope, granting me competence. These small moments, of learning Louis' acute care with the guidance of a careful nurse, made me feel capable as his mother.

These relationships taught me to surrender what I thought I knew of parenting, what I thought my baby's first year might look like. I learned to trust the advice of our care team. I needed them to share their knowledge and experience to teach me my next steps as a parent. With their support, I learned to push past the fear.

***

Dan and I slowly made our way to the eighth floor, knowing we were a few hours away from permission to enter Louis' room. Once we were off the elevator, the wide, double doors to the PICU were closed for an in-room procedure—no one allowed in or out of any of the rooms until Louis was stable. This helped to create a sterile field for the ECMO team.

Jon greeted us first in the PICU waiting room. Eager for his reassurance, seeing him relieved me. In earnest, he prepared us for what ECMO would look like at Louis' bedside. Jon led us back into the same room we had left half a day ago. Though Louis and his isolette had returned to their proper place, dozens of new tubes and monitors gathered, rendering the room unfamiliar. The two chairs Dan and I had been sleeping in had been replaced by a rolling cart with two monitors. It had a small metal box below that—a gauge regulating the temperature of Louis' blood. There were IV poles holding deep red cannulas—Louis' blood. These cannulas ran to the metal box, around a small plastic square labeled "LUNG," and disappeared into Louis' open chest covered by a sterile bandage and white linens. Unfamiliar beeps rang out as a new team of doctors and nurses managed the ECMO machine. With hardly any space to get close enough to touch Louis, the sight left me breathless.

The next person I saw was someone I had never met before. I watched her slide the door open just wide enough to slip into the room. She walked toward me with purpose, her somber expression made me sit upright. She said things like, "palliative care... here to make your stay more comfortable..." I couldn't remember her name.

Had she told me her name?

Who called her here?

What does palliative mean?

I studied every inch of her face; afraid it was telling me I wouldn't leave the hospital with my son. Her gentle demeanor and delicate voice told me that Louis was dying. I reached for the sink counter to steady myself, the only place there weren't people or machines. I couldn't consider that we might need it—palliative care. I wanted her to leave. I scanned the room for something familiar. The ECMO machine, so colossal, I couldn't look at it. I turned abruptly and staggered into the bathroom. The automatic light assaulted my senses as I entered. I leaned my back against the wall and let my body slide down the cold tile until I reached the floor. The reflections of city lights bounced off the window from the street down below. I could feel Dan standing beside me. For the first time, I began to pray.

"My god, my god, why have you forsaken me?"

That's all I could manage. I sat on the bathroom floor while half a dozen nurses hurried around the room. When I finally stood up, I heard Jon call my name. I stepped out of the bathroom and back into our reality. He stepped in front of me, called my name again and asked me to look at him.

Waiting for me to meet his gaze, he said, "It's okay. I've got him."

He put his hand on my shoulder and I couldn't stop the tears.

Still holding my gaze, he nodded sternly and repeated, "I've got him."

A day of research turned into a night of life saving. Morning had now arrived and unable to hold Louis or sit by his bedside, we reluctantly went home. Dan and I collapsed into bed wordless, holding our breath, hoping like hell the phone wouldn't ring. With the guarantee of morning rounds in just a few hours, we slept.

***

I woke a while later, without real rest, the sky still dark. I hadn't brushed my teeth and had slept in my jeans. I swung my legs out of bed and pushed myself up to stand. I shuffled my feet a few steps to the bathroom, opened the medicine cabinet for toothpaste, ran my brush under the faucet, and carried it to Louis' room. The nursery we had built for him was quiet and clean.

Each blanket, carefully folded and tucked away. The curtains pulled across the windows, making it safe and dark. The bookshelf stood tall, full of colorful stories; pages unread. A pile of stuffed animals hovered in the corner, tags still hanging from each ear and tail. He'd spent more time in the hospital than in this room.

I thought about my friends and what they might be doing with their babies at this hour. I felt a lightning bolt of jealousy. I let it linger on the tender part of my heart as I turned to leave my son's empty room. I rinsed my brush and spit in the sink. I remember voices advocating to stay positive, to look on the bright side. I couldn't. Or didn't want to. And I climbed back into bed.

When we arrived at the hospital the next morning, we were greeted by the new ECMO technician, Liam. Tall and broad shouldered, he looked like he had stepped off a rugby pitch. It felt appropriate that someone of his stature would control the herculean ECMO machine. I could hear music playing, classic rock, as we made our way to the sink. Liam had Bob Seger crooning from his computer, bringing an unexpected lightness to the room. He greeted us with enthusiasm and made sure he had our permission to keep playing "Kathmandu."

Liam hummed along to the music while Dan and I stood together awkwardly, surrounded by life support. We huddled next to each other, taking it all in. I took a deep breath and with it inhaled the scent of my freshly sanitized hands and hospital soap. I noticed a new sound, the whir of the ECMO machine. I swallowed my fear and asked a few questions. Liam explained every moving part. He reminded me that ECMO means Extracorporeal Membrane Oxygenation. He told me the details of each component's job, the role of every cord and wire and monitor—the tubing from Louis' chest, the cannulas, carried blood from his heart to a pump that did the work of the heart; an artificial lung did the work of oxygenating the blood, kind of like a heater and cooler to maintain proper temperature as the blood ran to and from all of these checkpoints, causing the machine's whirring. Two monitors watched blood pressure and checked levels of oxygen and carbon dioxide. Broken down into small scientific facts, this new information gave the fear less power. I wasn't intimidated anymore. I could look around the room. The fear of dying softened and became less immediate. Instead, I could see the healing around my son.

Hours of critical stability extended into days. Without chairs to sit in, Dan and I did our best to take turns milling around the hospital and checking in on Louis. We would spend a few hours huddled by his isolette reading chapter books we'd pulled from his bookshelf at home. Then we'd head back home for a nap or a meal—an intentional break from the ICU's intense environment. Days graduated into a week and a discussion of removing ECMO sparked. This meant they would clamp the cannulas connected to his heart to see if his body would circulate and maintain blood flow. It felt exciting and terrifying to talk about next steps. Louis was still so fragile. Considered a trial run, the removal required a sterile bedside procedure. We'd need to leave the room. They would treat his room like an operating room—

shutting down the PICU to visitors as our care team prepared clean hands, fresh gowns and sterile instruments like they would for surgery.

We were resigned to the lobby of the PICU where someone would update us with any news. They put a sign on the main entrance of the ICU that read, "STOP: SURGICAL PROCEDURE IN PROGRESS," to keep other PICU visitors out. No one would be allowed in or out of their room—patients, visitors, or care team, until the bedside procedure ended.

The process took more than an hour as they closely monitored Louis' heart and lungs regaining their responsibilities to oxygenate and pulse. A smaller, more private area in the waiting room sat off to the side near the elevators. A single door to enter, flanked by a long row of chairs on either side, faced a wall of windows that looked out over the city—much like the rooms of the PICU. This time, I tried to count pedestrians and how many times the stop light turned red. I couldn't occupy my mind or my hands. Dan and I sat together, quietly waiting.

When they finally updated us, a sense of calm spilled into the room. Louis tolerated the removal of the ECMO support enough for them to take it away completely. Although they would remove the heart and lung bypass, his chest would remain open due to swelling. Once the swelling went down, he would go back to the operating room to close his chest. We let out a partial sigh of relief. Louis was still critical, but more stable than the day before. That's all we could hope for.

Louis spent a few more days with his chest open, covered by a clear surgical bandage. At first, I requested the nurse keep his chest covered. Imagining his open chest made me physically weak. The more we leaned on his stability, the more I thought about what Louis might like to know once he was older. I asked the nurse to remove the receiving blanket covering his chest, underneath the breathing tube. I wanted to snap a few photos for his baby book. I might not be able to look at them for a while, but Louis might want to see someday. The nurse thought it a good idea, too. When I said ready, she methodically lifted the breathing tube and pulled the towel away while I stood at the foot of his isolette. It was mid-afternoon in the middle of winter. The sky looked as gray as Louis' skin. I held the camera to my eye and snapped away. Seeing a deep cavity spread open in the middle of my baby unnerved me. The pulse of his heart, learning to squeeze on its own, stood on display. Two tiny green wires entered his chest helping his heart's electrical signal. I watched the shadow in his chest jump at every pulse. I closed my eyes and reaffirmed the belief that Louis would want to know this moment. And then I asked her to put the towel back.

***

There were so many days I couldn't hold you. I would arrive at your room, everything the same as the day before. The door slid open a crack, indicating exclusive permission to anyone hoping to enter, the curtain pulled closed acting as a second gate to thwart off unwanted visitors, the lights dim, the window shades drawn to keep daylight at bay. Greeted first by the sink, the smell of soap, clean and sterile, filing the room. Compared to the hospital bed, your infant isolette took up less floor space but it also commanded the room—flanked by machines, anchored at the floor and ceiling, large electrical elements meant to provide respiratory support if you needed it. I didn't think you would need it.

Your tiny body in a warming isolette, a dozen cords running from your limbs to pumps and machines. Each machine wired to a screen, indicating medication quantities and timeline of administration. Your pillowcase was new. Laced with hockey sticks and pucks floating on icebergs. Your grandpa would like that. Dried blood on your skin, now wiped clean. Your bandages have been changed, their edges are squared and clean. The old bandages were lifting and curling at the corners, collecting fuzz from your blankets and our constant need to touch your skin.

The chairs shared the same fabric patterns, bright secondary colors, worn from the weary bodies who came before us. Near the outside wall, a floor-to-ceiling window looked out over downtown. While our world paused, the city buzzed below us like any other day. A cabinet on one wall, with a small countertop for us to stow our personal belongings, stayed littered with books and snacks, and family photographs. The opposite wall housed a door to our private bathroom entrance, a toilet and sink sharing the windowed wall.

The stitches of your PICC line and arterial IV still tugged at your skin, a layer of clear tape on top. The mechanical clicks of the ventilator, the rise and fall of your chest manufactured from machines—a comforting sound conveying your needs and confirming your stability. Your toes poked out from under your swaddle blanket—blankets I'd been sleeping with. I didn't want you to forget me.

Recovery

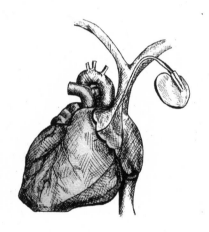

Dan and I trudged downstairs for breakfast after another restless night at home. Neither of us were sure how to start the day. We moved in quiet conversation. He grabbed a bowl but reconsidered before pouring the cereal. He put the bowl back in the cabinet and declared a preference for hospital food. I put an apple in my bookbag, knowing I wouldn't eat it later. As I inventoried my bag, the apple slid down to the bottom, settling alongside two paperback books—our next family read-aloud at Louis' bedside. I fumbled my hand around to search for my ChapStick and found a tiny container of homemade lotion. A gift from a friend. It smelled familiar, like frankincense and lavender and church—things I needed. I felt the tiny infant rosary bracelet made of teal silicone beads with a Madonna medallion that I had held onto the day Louis was born. I had turned it over and over in my hands during labor and delivery.

I zipped my backpack while Dan rinsed our coffee mugs. With a heavy sigh and nod of agreement, we headed out the door and down the steps. It had been nine weeks since my cesarean—major abdominal surgery. I hadn't rested like I was supposed to. Still tender, I safeguarded my belly, allowing my body to climb into the car.

Louis made steady improvements on ECMO, including noticeable recovery to his respiratory rate and blood pressures, but his electrical function hadn't returned. He was almost exclusively using the temporary pacing wires they had attached to the outside of his heart. He was gaining strength and it was time to close his chest, except his heart wouldn't beat on its own. I had learned, from Liam and ECMO, that asking questions helped quell my worry surrounding Louis' condition and care. I requested Dr. Haw to explain why a pacemaker was necessary.

"Well, I'm just the plumber," he said. "You need the electrician." And then he introduced us to Dr. Ratnysamy, an electrophysiologist. I asked *him* to explain it all again. He explained the miracle that is the electrical tissue of the heart, how the tissue sends a signal from the top of the heart saying, "PUMP," to the bottom of the heart that says, "FILL!"

Louis' heart was saying, "PUMP, PUMP, PUMP, PUMP... FILL," only filling about a quarter of the time. Dr. Ratnysamy introduced us to pacemakers—batteries that live inside the body, connected to the heart to complete the electrical signal. He would soon fit Louis for his atrial sensing, ventricular pacing pacemaker.

***

We arrived again at the 8th floor of the PICU. We waited with the receptionist while Louis' team performed a feeding tube change. We were allowed in after a few idle minutes. I stopped to wash my hands between the door and the rainbow privacy curtain. With one foot on the floor pedal, I squeezed the soap dispenser. Foam filled my hands. I began scrubbing my fingers and nails. The smell of soap had become jarring and familiar. The water became scalding hot and I felt grateful for the sensation to pull me from my thoughts. I lifted my foot to stop the water, tugged a few paper towels out and dried my hands.

Dan's turn.

While he scrubbed, I scanned the room for updates. I read the monitors: heart rate fast and still manually paced, blood pressure high, vent settings have lowered, he's started to breathe over the vent. My eyes moved across the room assessing the science, while my feet urged me close enough to kiss my baby's forehead. He smelled like Band-Aids, warm adhesive and sweat, sharp and sweet.

The shades were drawn; the room dark. Careful not to interrupt the nurses' conversation, I smiled at them. They met me with a soft, "Good morning, Mama. We were just talking—Louis wants you to hold him today. What do you think?"

I shifted my eyes away from them, trying not to cry. It had been several weeks since I'd held him. I stopped counting the days because it hurt too much. In an effort of self-preservation, I offered confirmation without commitment.

"I'll be here all day."

I didn't want to get my hopes up. Nearby commotion turned our attention to the door. Morning rounds had arrived. The team filed into the room.

I sat down in the oversized rocking chair I'd claimed as my own. Visibly worn in the seat, my body sank further down than I'd have liked. The headrest looked indented with worry, where countless other parents had sat, waiting for improvements in the health of their children. The two nurses began to untangle the lines and cords, methodical chaos that had me holding my breath. Dr. Brian stepped forward, filling the room with his presence, unassuming in his blue scrubs and white lab coat. He asked me if I'd like to hold Louis. All I could manage was a meager nod. He turned to the nurses with raised eyebrows, signaling approval. They finished their cord management and moved to opposite sides of the isolette. The first nurse scooped Louis up—one hand under his head and the other under his bottom, the second nurse managed cords to the ventilator and PICC line on his left while a third stepped in to hold the lines on his right side. They walked over to me like they were holding a cake lit with birthday candles. Slowly and gently, they lowered Louis into the crook of my left arm and continued the dance of cord management around us.

The intensivist reached for the top of Louis' head and said, "You hold him as long as you want today, Mom." I searched for the words to thank him, but I couldn't speak. I felt the tears streaming down my cheeks and hoped my face conveyed my wordless gratitude.

I had yet to learn the maternal needs of my baby. Holding him was restoration for the both of us. We sat statue-still in that rocking chair until the sun went down, together. Love grew when nothing else was certain.

Through the waiting, I'd been acutely focused on survival, setting my sights on every single mundane task, centering small moments to avoid the feelings I'd hidden somewhere between fear and hope—both too terrifying to question. We were stretched thin, met with a lull, until we were forced to stretch again, more each time. It wasn't strength that brought us there. It was resilience. I was reminded of the prayer my grandma had shared with me.

> *Do not pray for easy lives, pray to be stronger people. Do not pray for tasks equal to your powers; pray for powers equal to your tasks.* — *Father Solanus Casey*

I wrote it down and tacked it to the door of Louis' hospital room. One of the fellows studying to become an PICU intensivist, Dr. Danny, noticed it first. I thought he was just being nice, but he commented, "Fr. Solanus, I like it, and to put it on the door—the doorkeeper, clever." I hadn't made the connection myself. His knowledge of Fr. Solanus felt like a sign of divine care.

I used tiny threads like this to build hope, to quiet the fear in my heart. If sheer will be the only factor, no hospitals would be needed. Parents and partners would simply resolve their loved ones to wellness. I walked the halls with parents fighting for their children. I sat in waiting rooms with grandparents praying for their grandkids. I watched siblings celebrate their own birthdays at bedsides, holding their family together.

If he dies; I die.

In the moments I felt farthest away from hope, I

turned further away from faith. I was reminded of a quoted passage from a book by Mother Teresa:

"In the darkness... Lord, my God, who am I that You should forsake me? ...You have thrown away as unwanted—unloved. I call, I cling, I want—and there is no One to answer—no One on Whom I can cling— no, No One.— Alone... Where is my Faith—even deep down right in there is nothing, but emptiness & darkness—My God— how painful is this unknown pain—I have no Faith—I dare not utter the words and thoughts that crowd in my heart—& make me suffer untold agony."

I thought of Mother Teresa as someone who carried a great light in this world. To know that such a faithful woman also carried a deep-seated doubt comforted me. That faith and fear could coexist gave me permission to pray in a way that worked for me.

***

I kept myself busy by decorating Louis' hospital room. I hung pictures near his bed. I taped an E.E. Cummings poem to the wall:

i carry your heart with me (i carry it in
my heart) i am never without it (anywhere
i go you go, my dear; and whatever is done
by only me is your doing, my darling)

i fear
no fate (for you are my fate, my sweet) i want

no world (for beautiful you are my world, my true)
and it's you are whatever a moon has always meant
and whatever a sun will always sing is you

here is the deepest secret nobody knows
(here is the root of the root and the bud of the bud
and the sky of the sky of a tree called life; which grows
higher than soul can hope or mind can hide)
and this is the wonder that's keeping the stars apart

i carry your heart (i carry it in my heart)

During a routine visit to our room, one of the intensivists, Dr. Chris, recognized the poem. He shared that he and his wife had put it on their wedding programs. He asked if we had heard of Michael Hedges, a musician who created a song with this poem as lyrics. We hadn't, so he looked it up. We all had tears in our eyes while we watched a short video clip of this musician I'd never heard of. Energized by this connection, he walked over to our nurse Alyssa and gave her a knowing look. Earlier that week I had asked her what brought her to study nursing. She told us that this hospital treated her for cancer during her high school days. She wanted to give the same care that they had given her. Her compelling story surprised me and I felt grateful for her sincere, empathetic care.

These little connections kept showing up. It felt like every person had been hand-picked to care for Louis, including me. Needing a full care team for my newborn had broken me down. It humbled me, but it has also taught me how to be a mother: selfless, grateful and, completely exhausted. His care team taught me gratitude in unexpected ways.

Louis' recovery had to start over. We got to start over. I felt the constant dithering between deep sadness and endless gratitude. Unequipped to provide our son's care on our own, yet supported by the skill and knowledge of a dozen caregivers.

A few more weeks in the hospital taught us about the specific care he needed, different than anything I'd imagined: syringe feeds, nasogastric tube changes, medication administration. Slowly we moved farther away from the crisis—out of the PICU and into a regular hospital room while we regained competence. We stayed inpatient for several weeks, taking turns at Louis' bedside to manage his care overnight. My first night in the hospital, he threw up his syringe feeding around midnight. Every muscle in my body tensed. The familiar worry. It knew my name and recognized my face. We'd been here before. Louis had thrown up two other times—once during his heart check-up that landed us in the ICU, and a second time when we called 911. I held my breath and whispered Hail Mary's while the nurse checked his vitals. I couldn't trust myself to help him—not yet. The memory of his delicate frame turning gray still haunted me. I needed her reassurance while teaching me how to give the care he needed.

We accepted the new hardware in Louis' abdomen—tiny round wires securing his split sternum, more wires still anchored to his heart and winding down between his rib cage, resting in a battery at his belly.

Pulsing.

Pumping.

We changed the function of his heart.

Motherhood

Feeling less naïve with some wisdom edging in, we brought Louis home again. He looked tired and delicate, but so pink this time! Dr. Heather kept saying Louis reset the clock. Now we would relearn everything a baby needed to learn—how to eat, when to sleep, and in a few weeks, he would learn how to move after open-heart surgery.

At one time, I had a list of parenting best practices: cloth diapering, no pacifiers, breastfeeding over formula. I'd make my own baby food. Absolutely no co-sleeping. The list was long and none of it included considerations for life-saving measures. Those decisions became glaringly more important. Those decisions were for survival. Our reality made that original list insignificant. I adjusted my expectations and surrendered to medicine.

I changed my mind.

If he lived through this heart surgery, he could eat whichever way kept him growing. If we could bring him home, he'd sleep anywhere I could see the rise and fall of his chest.

Several steps were needed before we could go home, all to make sure we were competent parents. Soon, my turn to place the NG tube arrived. NG means nasoga-stric—through the nose, past the throat, and into the stomach. I watched the nurse do it every six days—stretching the tube from the earlobe to the nose, from the nose to the end of his sternum, measuring how far it needs to go to reach his stomach. No longer in an isolette, the hospital bed had crib rails lowered on either side to give us full access to his tiny frame. The nurse stood on one side, opening and organizing the supplies: the thin orange tube; a little pad of lubricant so the end of the tube slides into his nose; three narrow ribbons of tape to secure it once the tube is placed; two clear Tegaderm dressings to cover the ends of the tape on his cheeks. None of these items were on the baby registry. We swaddled Louis to keep him still, needing calm and stillness or this wouldn't work. Palms sweaty, I mea-sured twice—repeating the steps out loud for audible approval.

"OK Mom, once you push the NG through, take an empty syringe to the end of the feeding tube and pull it back," she began. "If it fills with air, that means the NG is in his lungs and we need to pull it out and try again. If you pull back fluid that's bile in the stomach—success! We can tape the end to his cheek and you won't have to do it again for another week!"

NG tube measured, syringe ready like we're sitting at the top of a rollercoaster as it slowly ticks to the top, threatening to tip over the edge, I pushed the NG through his nose past his throat. To my horror, the tube went into his nose and came surging out of the roof of his mouth. He must have been taking a tremendous inhale when

I started. He wriggled out of his blanket, arms flailing about like he was drowning.

Right then, I imagined other moms at home holding their babies, carefree, dancing around their living rooms.

"It's OK," she said, recognizing the defeat on my face. "You didn't hurt him. Sometimes that happens, we can try again when you're ready."

I learned what type of tape irritated his skin as we secured the feeding tube to his cheeks. I learned how to listen to the difference between his heartbeat and his inhale with a stethoscope. I learned to trust the visiting nurse and physical therapists. I asked the nutritionist and occupational therapist questions when they came for biweekly home visits. They showed me how to introduce solid foods and how to feed Louis to reduce the amount of vomiting— frequent breaks with gentle burping. I would teeter him on my knee in a seated position, cradling his chin in my hand and firmly rub his back until he burped.

"How To Manage Newborn Sternal Precautions or Pacemaker & Your 3 Month Old"— milestones that weren't in the baby books. My parenting style went from a checklist of dos and don'ts to simple gratitude. We celebrated our progress, even when it included additional chest tube drains for postoperative bleeding or withdrawal symptoms from fentanyl.

Inside the hospital, progress wasn't measured by dates on the calendar but by the body's ability to gain strength.

I lost track of days and instead stared at my baby, memorizing the contours of his sweet physical being, powerless over the fear that each time I held him might be the last. Paralyzed and sedated by medication, I had seen Louis' heart beating in his open chest. Tubes and wires gathered in every direction; I had been afraid to touch him. I had spent those few months in the hospital worried I wouldn't get to know his personality, when all along he had shown us how delicate and fierce he was.

I don't think it was luck and I'm not sure about miracles, mostly because not every deserving person gets one. It is science and wonder and Louis. Motherhood has taught me that life is more than sharing the feel-good moments. We wouldn't know the depth of Louis' hardiness without acknowledging the pieces that made us fall apart, his frailties. I can see now that Louis was born of resilience. His first year of life sang a song of strength through vulnerability. We wouldn't have found one without the other. I honor every step because it brought us together as a family and gave us a healthy growing boy, whose heart is kind and sweet and needs a battery to beat.

***

My first mommy and me playgroup consisted of Louis and me and his physical therapist, PT Lisa. I always called her "PT Lisa" to avoid confusing her with my best friend. PT Lisa came over once a week and allowed me to normalize my experience as a mother while supporting me in learning what my son needed next. I could tell her about Louis' history, and she didn't recoil in horror or tilt her head in sympathy. She listened and she empowered us both, Louis and me, to work together to reach our goals. Tummy time over mama's leg several times a day to soften the pressure on his chest. Rolling a blanket behind him to keep him side-lying to offset his stiff neck muscles. For months, I looked forward to PT Lisa's visits. She became my first friend born of motherhood. As Louis regained strength, our visits spread out and trickled to a stop. On her final visit to the house, words weren't enough. I gave Lisa a philodendron and did my best to thank her on a 4x6-sized thank you note. I cried from the front porch as she drove away, while I held my rolling, crawling, giggling baby. Louis—a glowing success story of her consistent care, and she—a friend I didn't know I needed in a time I felt desperately isolated. At times during that first year, Dan and I didn't talk much about the future because we were busy surviving. Now I needed to plant my feet firmly in the present. It was too overwhelming to imagine long-term scenarios when every moment brought a breathtaking obstacle. I put one foot in front of the other as we moved farther away from survival and closer to stability.

During one quiet and uneventful night, after we had moved out of the PICU, a few questions bounced around in my mind. I approached the nurses' station for their insight. They sent some of our PICU nurses, Hayley and Jon, down to our floor. I was delighted to see them in a situation where we weren't in need of their care. I smiled, jumping right into my complex thoughts on blood and the body, and they were equally delighted. Hayley answered my questions, then added, "I am so proud of you.

Here you are weathering this hospital stay and I'm not pulling you off the ceiling this time."

I had felt like a worried mom all the time. I hadn't considered that my growth would have been so obvious. But here I was, shoulder to shoulder with my partner, tilling up information to empower me as a caregiver. I thought about what Hayley said all night as I watched my son breathing on his own, resting in his hospital bed. I had come a long way, too. All worth celebrating.

Eventually, this knowledge and experience allowed me to see hope and longevity, to envision birthdays and Christmases. Dan and I slowed down our lives to start appreciating the normal and mundane things: our first dinner at home with Louis in his highchair, our first date leaving Louis with a babysitter (this one took a while), our first family vacation across the country to Big Sky, Montana, where Louis learned to crawl and Dan and I went white water rafting. We were finding our footing outside the hospital and tending to our needs as a family.

Celebrating our milestones got us thinking about how best to honor the mending of Louis' heart. We decided to commemorate our family by getting married.

PART V

Marriage

When I was five months pregnant with Louis, I went to the bridal salon alone. Enthusiastic brides, separated by mountains of white tulle and lace, filled the shop. A professional woman, dressed in all black, approached me. She asked how many people were in my party and if I had made a reservation.

No, just me.

I told her my budget. I could see her disappointment. I told her I knew what I didn't want—anything over the top. She asked more questions: silk or lace, white or champagne, ballgown or mermaid. I had no idea. I thought my lack of preference would make me a blank canvas, but I could see she had a hard time finding a dress that didn't come with any of those extras.

I tried on three dresses, sweating over the shape of my body and its impending changes in the coming months. I made a mental note to size up. The first dress was a shell of lace from neck to waist, waist to ankle. I looked like the bride of Frankenstein. PASS. The next one flowed with silk and a slender cut that showed every bodily imperfection, doing nothing for my self-esteem. One more dress, a sleeveless lace underneath a soft layer of tulle, looked subtle and understated. I snapped a quick unflattering photo in the 360° mirror of each dress, sending all three to my mom. She replied immediately—she liked whichever one I liked.

You're supposed to go gaga over every nuptial detail, mimosas and bridesmaids with big opinions, matching linens with dresses and boutonnieres, mood boards full of wedding must-haves, and flower arrangements. I didn't. The idea of being the center of attention made me want to run screaming in the opposite direction. Looking at myself in the mirror, draped in dresses made for fairy tales, made me squirm. I returned to the dressing room, put my jeans back on, and threw all three dresses back on their hangers. The saleswoman wrote down the dresses I tried on in case I changed my mind. I left the store empty-handed, defeated. I wanted to get married. I wanted to celebrate with my family and friends, but I did not want the fuss. Fancy dresses, seating charts, and menu options all felt too demanding.

I called my mom from the car. We decided I looked more comfortable in the third dress with the sleeveless lace and tulle. I ordered it a few days later over the phone. Without a wedding date on the calendar, I brought it home and shoved it in the back of our attic closet where it would sit for nearly two years. I put the rest of the wedding planning on hold. It was too much. We could pick it up after we had our baby. I had no idea we would spend that year focused on survival.

Ready to get married with a stable Louis at home, we deserved a celebration. Though we proved to be a fierce team committed to our family, I wanted a formal proclamation to celebrate our partnership, no longer about correcting the order of things. It was about our commitment to each other, which didn't belong to anyone but us. It became an occasion to celebrate the incredible resilience of our brave boy and the loyal and supportive bond we had forged through his health ordeal. Standing as bride and groom had felt superficial before. Now, the ceremony felt necessary and important.

Wedding planning brought renewed excitement. Instead of focusing on how things looked, we reflected on how we felt. As I combed through the calendar in early spring, I recounted Louis' hospital baptism and the anniversary of his emergency heart surgery. Memories can sometimes be a torturous reminder of where you've been. They can also bring relief. The Tenth of November, and the days surrounding it, carry sorrow and fear with commitment and new beginnings—the roots of our family tree. We celebrated our joy and resilience in holy matrimony on that day, honoring a date originally filled with worry and fear.

I dug into wedding planning by eliminating details that didn't hold meaning, such as boutonnieres. We traded an Hors D'oeuvres hour for two kegs of Neapolitan stout. We hired a jazz band instead of a DJ and offered donuts instead of cake. We picked a reception venue that gave a bird's eye view of the city—the Bissell Tree House.

Nestled into the hillside, with the children's hospital visible at the peak of the skyline. We asked Father G, who had baptized Louis in the hospital, to complete the sacrament during our wedding ceremony.

Six months before our wedding, we began our marriage preparation with counseling courses at the church. When Father G asked about my faith, I came up empty-handed. I admitted my faith had been tested and hadn't survived the fallout of Louis' journey. He recommended a book: *Where the Hell is God?* Bewildered that such a title existed and that my priest was recommending it, I found an out-of-print copy and ordered it right away.

Where the Hell is God is a Jesuit priest's reflection of his own personal suffering. It's not an account of theological studies or overtly positive platitudes. It is honest, self-reflexive, and exactly what I needed to hear within the faith family I felt so ostracized by.

> *"God does not directly send pain, suffering, and disease.*
> *God does not punish us.*
> *God does not send accidents to teach us things, though we can learn from them.*
> *God's will is more in the big picture than in the small stuff."*

And that's just in the preface. His story of suffering, relatable and heart-wrenching, granted me permission to be both a good Catholic and a good mother—giving space for doubt and fear and unconditional love.

Father G gave us a compatibility test with questions on finance, career goals, and family planning. Dan and I answered them individually without discussion. Father G went through our questions one at a time. When variation on expectation occurred, he encouraged us to engage in discussion together. When I answered the questions, I assumed the results would be pass/fail, but it was all about cooperation. He taught us that compromise provided the key to longevity.

In these counseling sessions, I refused to look beyond the hardship we'd already weathered. Nothing would be more challenging than facing our child's survival rate. We were lucky our experience hadn't torn us apart. We learned to talk about uncomfortable things, to share our most vulnerable feelings before we felt stretched beyond our limits.

Parenthood fueled our partnership and the way we worked together as a team. Our first year as parents forced a type of fast forward in our relationship. We learned how to speak up and when to ask questions. We learned to say what we were feeling and to really listen to what the other had to say. The compatibility test reinforced all that we had learned—it's okay to disagree, keep sharing concerns, and talk about it. Communication is important.

Instead of pulling the other up, pushing for a bright side, we sat down next to each other giving dark feelings their space. We allowed room for all of it—the bright and the unbearable, to become a stronger team more equipped for parenthood.

I felt more nervous wearing a white dress, with so many people looking at me, than I was about the responsibility of marriage. We already made our commitment, a foundation that had been tested as partners and parents. Getting married? Just a formality.

WITH THE BLESSING OF THEIR PARENTS
MR & MRS WILLIAM RIBBENS
AND
MR & MRS MICHAEL BATCHIK
REQUEST THE HONOR OF YOUR PRESENCE AT THE
MARRIAGE OF THEIR CHILDREN
DANIEL DeWITT RIBBENS
&
NICOLE ANN BATCHIK
AND THE BAPTISM OF LOUIS DeWITT RIBBENS
ON FRIDAY THE TENTH OF NOVEMBER AT 2:30 IN
THE AFTERNOON
AT THE CATHEDRAL OF ST ANDREWS IN GRAND
RAPIDS, MICHIGAN
DINNER AND DANCING TO FOLLOW

Our wedding day celebrated our partnership and fidelity to one another, along with the bravery and baptism of our darling Louis. We spent that morning at home. The house bustled with excitement and family members made breakfast and ironing shirts. Air mattresses in the guest room and fresh towels in the bathroom. I poured myself a second cup of coffee and as I made my way to the attic for hair and makeup, I stopped on the steps to take a listen. Our home, one that had felt big and empty while we waited to bring Louis home, now full of laughter and chaos and people, and a healthy napping baby— growing stronger every day.

We took our time most of the morning, only to arrive at the church to realize no one had the rings, delaying the entire ceremony. My dad drove back to the house to get them. Dan held Louis as he walked down the aisle. I hid a baby bottle in my bouquet as I walked down the aisle, arm in arm with both my parents. My grandmother played Clair de Lune on the church piano with my grandfather as her official page-turner. Dan and I kissed Louis and handed him and the bottle to my mom, seated in the front row. We shared our vows, and both of our dads prayed over us. We completed Louis' baptismal rite, one we started a year before fearing his death, this time exalting in his life. We signed our marriage certificate with strict instructions from Father G to get them to the proper office Monday morning or we would have to do this all over again.

Our photographer ushered Dan and me to a nearby parking structure. We had our wedding party with us, Lisa and Rose, to take some photos at the top of the garage. It was early November. We carefully stepped through the snow collecting on the cement. I hadn't planned for a winter coat. We took a few candid photos overlooking the city before heading to dinner.

We drove to the reception and took the trolley up to the hilltop high above—a beautiful sunset skyline with the Children's hospital smiling back at us from the center of town. A stark contrast to the memories of the year before. Dan and I agree our favorite memory of the night had to be watching my grandparents behaving like newlyweds on the dance floor, swinging to jazz music like no one was watching. I can't remember what we had for dinner but I do remember the thrill of being first in line for a drink any time we wanted one, and watching our friends eating donuts on the dance floor, and holding Louis between us—the picture of health after a turbulent year. The whole experience marked a change in the tide, allowing us to exhale, giving room for hope.

We planned a brunch at a local restaurant for our visiting friends and family the next day. A morning of hot coffee and an all-you-can-eat breakfast buffet, a chance to visit before they all went back home. Once we filled our bellies and said our goodbyes, we paid the bill while the restaurant boxed our leftovers. My parents came back home with us and my mom took Louis up to his room for a nap. Dan and I collapsed on the couch in the living room. The first quiet moment of the weekend.

"This was the right way," my dad said unexpectedly to both of us. He sat down on the opposite end of the L-shaped couch.

"I thought you should have gotten married before the baby came," he continued. "I didn't understand why you wouldn't do that. But I see now that this was the right way—to wait and to celebrate on your terms."

He hugged us both, finally dissolving the tangle of misunderstanding between us.

Grief

Grieving can happen without death. We mourned the shift in our expectations, in the life we thought we'd have. When an experience has rewired our brains, we often call it heartbreak, disrupting functions of the body: how we sleep, how we react to stress, how we relax. Our hearts are strong, but we hold memories triggered by experience. The fear of recurrence seeps through the cracks. When a life-limiting diagnosis occurs, it introduces chronic sorrow. Each time a new limitation is discovered, a new boundary firmly placed, you'll grieve the loss all over again.

For me, fear came first and some days, it was all I could muster. It started as denial and jealousy—that I wouldn't have newborn firsts like everyone else. I rejected the steps from the doctor, a scheduled C-section, waiting for Louis to show distress before surgery. I wanted to keep my baby safe in my belly. Toxic platitudes and empty encouragements rang hollow and fueled my anger. Feeling angry at God or myself meant no room left to be let down. Fear and frustration became my safety net. Worry became my comfort. I knew a gratitude list wouldn't stop anything bad from happening.

It's easy to stir up grief from memory. My brain holds a vice grip on the fear. But I am reminded of what Louis has overcome as he sings for a popsicle and shares his snacks with the dog. The grief melts a little on those days, revealing endless opportunities in his life. Some days, I can't believe it ever happened. Other days, it's still all I feel or hear or see.

Knowing Louis is both art and science. I want to be sure my diligence spans all the Earth for answers for him. The past is not in the rearview. Sometimes it feels like it's a window to what's next. It's not easy to wipe away the residue left behind. We'll never rule out the possibility of more surgery or a heart transplant—those risks always loom. Every breath he takes is its own tiny miracle. I remember it all in my body, a visceral recollection of heartache. I take comfort knowing he won't have any memory of this except for the external scars, both tough and tender.

Scar tissue isn't sure where to grow, so it binds around bones like tentacles. We learned how to give Louis scar massages, to soften the scar tissue, unbinding it from his bones. The nurses taught us that with time and massage, the scars would fade. Foreign at first, afraid to hurt him—I gently began by kneading circles over Louis' sternum. Tight in the center, tethered to wires twisted under his skin, pulling his bone together. As a baby, he remained unbothered by the massage. Each time growing more comfortable, I would press more firmly, feeling the tissue loosen under the skin. Now, at four years old, he sometimes asks for a scar massage as he falls asleep at night.

Like grief, sometimes the touch of his chest jolts my memory back to survival mode, and I begin to fret over what else may be asked of him.

Memory

Fear of the unknown surged while waiting for Louis' initial surgery. It came again when carrying him to an ambulance. And a third time, when doctors whisked him away to reopen his tiny chest—moving from urgent to lifesaving as evening turned to morning. His second surgery, fraught with complications, left me feeling fragile. I made an inventory of what unexpected things might threaten us next—fearing what I couldn't predict. I pushed through the day, one chore at a time: wake up, brush teeth, get dressed.

Single tasks eventually turned to days as Louis grew stronger. Our days at home were marked with visits by home health care aids teaching Louis the fundamentals of babyhood and me how to support him here. The fog slowly lifted and somehow, we muddled through the next string of days. Amid all this hardship, I felt gratitude growing during those vulnerable moments. But I couldn't explain any of it without acknowledging the grief. Grief and gratitude became partners. Resilience bloomed when I allowed them to coexist.

I can't remember what was important to me before all of this.

It's a dream to watch him breathe and pulse and sleep. Louis' belly resembles a battlefield—scars and valleys that tell a turbulent story of days spent fighting to live. I am reminded of the intentional preservation of our family, from science and technology and kind hearts, each time he wakes in the night, or when my alarm sounds for another medication time.

When the house is quiet, I can still hear the monitors beeping. When we drive downtown, the hospital is no longer an anonymous mirrored building—I drive by, and I see my reflection on the other side. A new mother, full of worry, looking for details she hadn't noticed before, searching desperately for a sign to hold on to. A butterfly, a flower, a familiar face—hope.

***

Louis is four years old. One evening, while playing with the kids next door, he tripped in the driveway. Already crying before he got himself up off the ground and bleeding from his face, he wiped his nose and mouth yelling, "It hurts! It really hurts!" Blood pooled between his upper lip and nose. "It hurts so bad!" he yelled as I picked him up carefully, unsure of other injuries. He wrapped his arms and legs around me as I carried him into the house. Dan was already at the sink, wetting a paper towel. I cleaned his face, reassuring him his safety. He cried out, "Maybe a popsicle! A popsicle will make me feel better."

He held onto me while sitting on the kitchen counter. I scooped him up and Dan followed us into the family room. Sitting in my lap, Louis started to calm down. He let me get a good look at his mouth and lip. The bleeding slowed, showing a deep vertical cut above his top lip. He needed stitches. We took the drive to the emergency department. I climbed out of the backseat and greeted the security guard while unbuckling Louis from his car seat. The emergency department was only allowing one caregiver with each child, so Dan dropped us off and went to the store to buy all of Louis' favorite frozen treats. I promised to update him when we met with the doctor.

Once inside, they escorted us to our own room. The doctor introduced herself and looked over Louis' injury. Bruised gums but nothing broken, a few stitches would fix him up. Louis wouldn't sit anywhere but in my lap. Each time someone new came into the room, he whimpered and snuggled closer to me. We were comfortable that way.

The doctor made small talk as she put on her gloves. She moved toward Louis with gauze in one hand and a syringe full of saline in the other. She held the gauze up to Louis' lip as she cleaned out the blood and dirt and gravel with saline. Louis held my thumbs, but he didn't flinch. He slurped up the saline as it dripped past the gauze. He declared, "mmm...YUMMM!" He loves salty things—saline is no exception.

I realized that we were in the hospital and I hadn't once worried about Louis' heart or his survival. We were not scared.

"It tastes like ketchup with pickles!" he said, and we imagined other gross food combinations, pancakes with mustard, relish and ice cream. His laughter eased the anxiety for both of us. The doctor swapped her syringe for a small, curved needle and thread. With gloved hands, a nurse held Louis' head still. He clenched my thumbs tighter. The doctor leaned in and told Louis this would be quick. As she pushed the needle through his skin he started to cry.

The Purell and saline, mixed with blood and tears and sweat. The adhesive of a new bandage and bleached linen. The scent of Louis' first year. I saw the small, rounded needle poke through the flesh of his upper lip, guiding the string through, gently pulling his gashed skin together.

The tingling smell of survival rose to greet me, alarming and familiar.

I held Louis' hands while he cried and screamed, "I don't love this! Let's go home, Mama!"

I felt warm tears run down my face. The nurse caught my eye and I felt her sympathy. "We've been through so much," I whimpered, embarrassed.

I couldn't stop the tears. The blood, the stitches, the sweat. All the things I am not able to protect him from. I am forced to remain on the sidelines. I try like hell to understand and advocate, but I have no idea how he feels.

One, two, three, the doctor finished the stitches.

"Let's leave, Mama!" Desperation in his voice. The doctor showed me the neat stitches before she bandaged him up. Louis curled in my lap, careful not to bump his face. I was grateful he felt safety in my physical presence. I am the refuge. I can't always keep the hard stuff away, but I can be the safe harbor for mending.

He is only four-years-old.

It was only three stitches.

We made it home in time for bed. He snuggled in with his hands wrapped around my fingers. I rested my right hand on his belly. The indentations of his scars, familiar terrain under my fingertips. His chest healed unevenly—higher on the left side, with lines and stitches of necessity like a treasure map, marking his first open-heart surgery, his second, his pacemaker implantation, his chest tubes, and his peritoneal drain. There are more, still, tiny bumps near his shoulder from his PICC line stitches and at his wrist from the arterial line. All of them were created with intention—to save his life. His scar tissue spreads like tree roots under the surface of his growing body. It's a lot like memory, forgotten specifics still charting moments in time, shaping his future. These scars render hurdles we worked hard to overcome and then were asked to leap over again. And again.

We were halfway through *This Old Man* before the sting of my tears surprised me. Louis was quiet. His eyelids grew heavy as he settled into his pillow. He exhaled a whispered hum and fell fast asleep. I memorize these moments, an effort to find my way, preparing for our next obstacle.

There is only one way and it's through. It's not glamorous or neat—it's messy and beautiful. We keep pushing, hoping that the bounty at the end means more living.

Acknowledgements

I began writing to catalog Louis' story before his memory began. As I put pen to paper, I realized these experiences defined who I am as a mother. To tell Louis his story, I had to tell mine first—and the rest unfolded. To simply say, "thank you," would never be enough, but I still must share my gratitude: To Dan, my partner, for sharing the fear and heartache and finding ourselves together on the other side, stronger and united in whatever comes next. A constant encouragement in following my heart. Cornbread and butterbeans and you across the table.

To Jojo and Boppa, for filling in the gap with time and care, house projects and Legos, and to Bill and Martha, for leading with excitement and support, and candy corn.

This book would have remained sentence fragments in my nightstand notebook if it weren't for my team at The Self-Publishing Agency. Megan & Ira—your experience and guidance on all things vulnerable.

I believe in the scissors more than I do the pencil, Truman Capote says. Tara, with your skill, my story was revealed. Thank you for being my scissors. Julie, for all the commas and em dashes and grammar advice. Your attention to detail helps me feel like I've put my best foot forward with my story. Petya, for taking my manuscript and illustration files and turning it into a real book. Adam, your ability to read between the lines to create a visual representation of what's in my heart is unparalleled. Holly, for illustrating our superhero son and giving sight to our story with your illustrations. Thanks for petitioning my parents to keep me in public schools all those years ago.

To Lisa and Raquel, for always allowing me the safety and comfort to grieve and cry and sing in mothering. My team of heart moms, I am humbled to live this life alongside you and your beautifully resilient children. Our stories overlap but diverge on different paths. I draw strength and compassion from each one of you.

Lastly but most importantly, we give thanks to our medical care team—Heather Sowinski, Amy Neumann, Marcus Haw, Joseph Vettukattil, Chris Ratnasamy, Neal Hillman, Giedruis Baliulis, Annette Weston, Bryan Boville, Chris DeBano, Danny, Amy, Abby, Sarah, Sarah, Sara, Alyssa, Jon, Kayla, Haley, Chad, Jordan, David, PT Lisa and Nutritionist Lisa. You all brought the care Louis needed to survive and the support I needed to become the fierce mother I am now. You turned our fear into education and understanding. I see your faces each time Louis does something new, and he lights up with pride.

The story of Louis, the story of mothering through congenital heart disease, continues to evolve. The need for medical support ebbs and flows. For now, we are home and huddling for rest, building our reserve for the next time resilience will be asked of us. Waves of fear and gratitude crash the shore every day, reminding me that now is most important. We'll get there when we get there, and not a moment sooner. And we will sing our sweet Louis' praise the whole way through.